AF488342

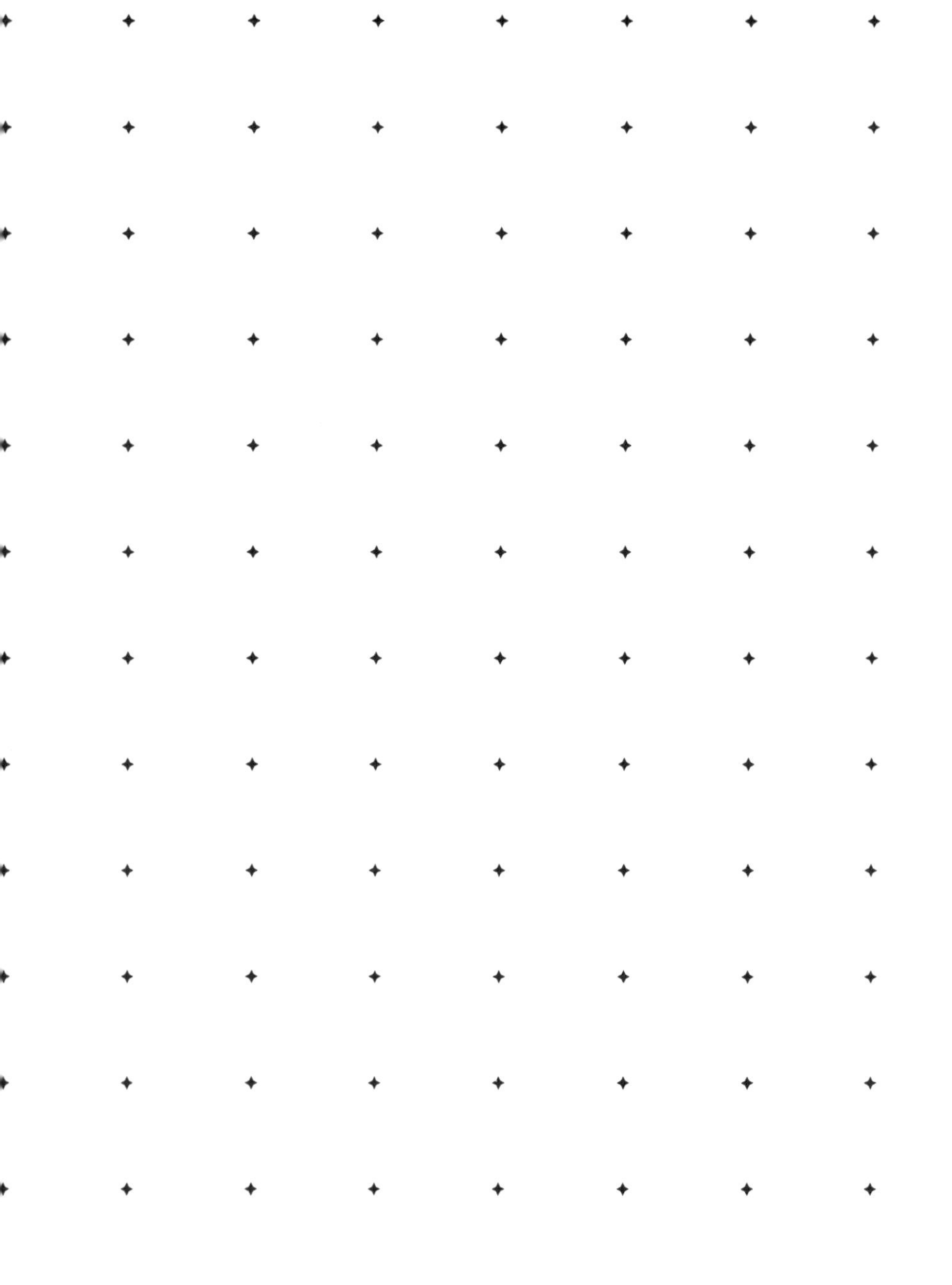

THE SURRENDER OF MAN

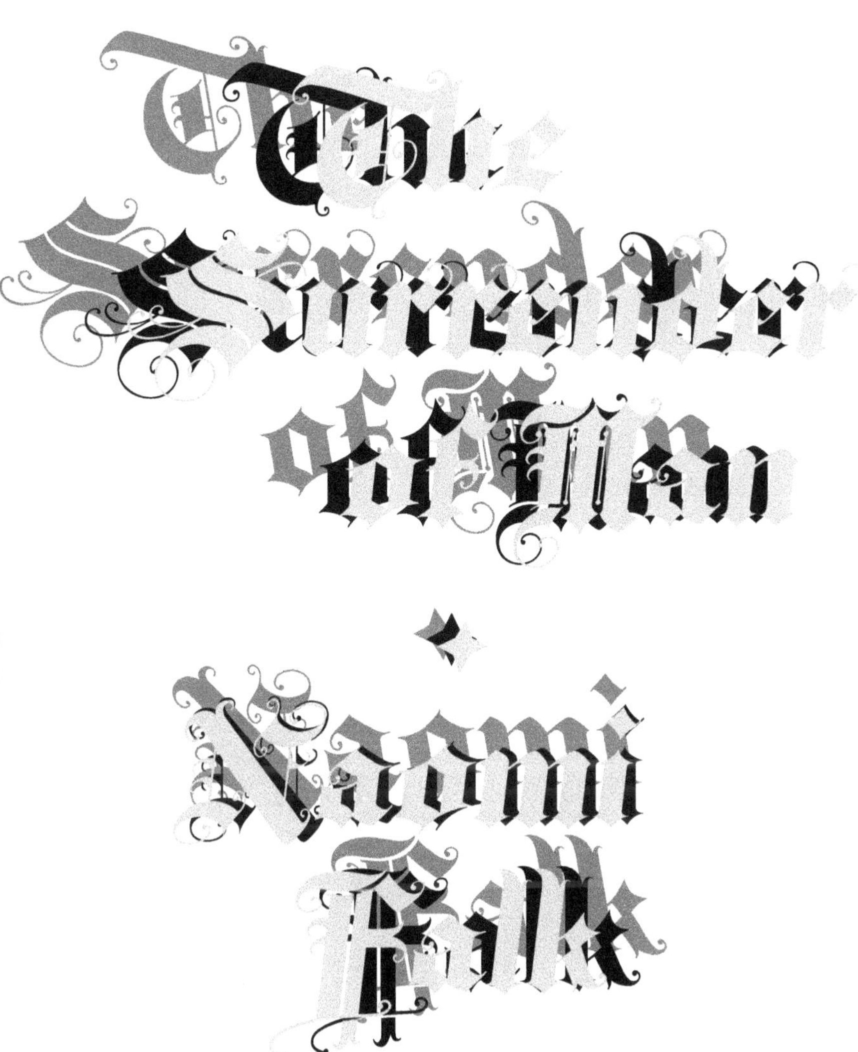

The Surrender of Man

Naomi Falk

ISBN: 979-8-989550-05-0

The Surrender of Man is typeset in Janson Text, a digital facsimile created by Hermann Zapf in 1954. The font's name comes from the mid-17th century dutch printer, Anton Janson, who the type's origins are falsely attributed to. In actuality, its design can be traced back to Miklos Kis, a Transylvanian schoolmaster who was known to cut letters for the Georgian king, Archil of Imereti.

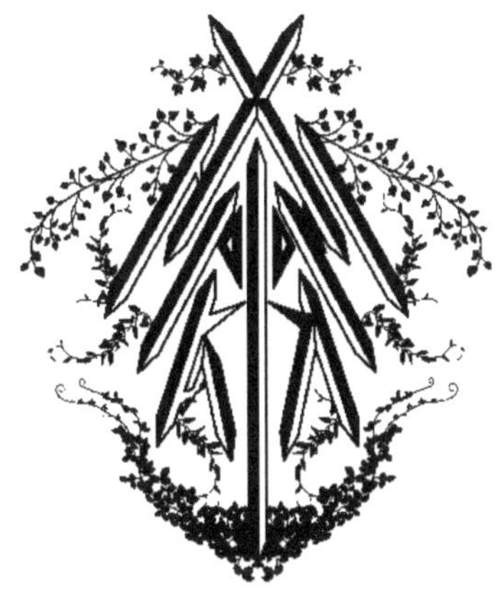

For Beverly Terry

"Bury me deep enough that the earth/ will push me
into something new."

— Chukwuma Ndulue
"Sacrifices at the Altar of the Chicken"

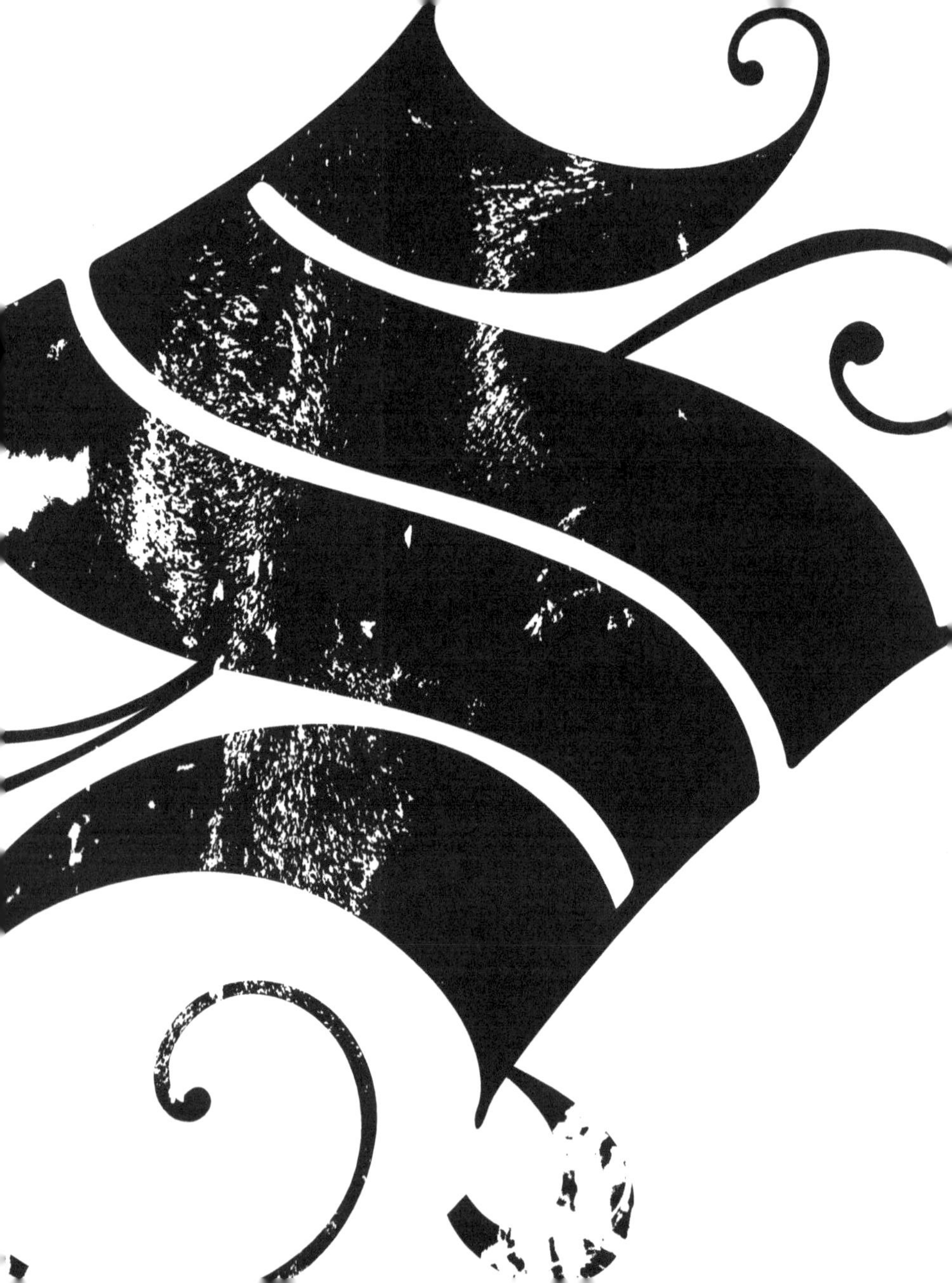

PROLOGUE

In moments of darkness, I gravitate toward art.
Like a desperate magnet, I cling to that which keeps me of the world. A writer tells of the time she passes in the presence of a work of art and, in turn, unfurls static into the air. Each surface I encounter thus becomes shocking, forcing me into new feelings. I aim to discover what it means to experience my life outside the jading shackles of apathy.

Objects possess transformative potential when you look closely, fastened by their makers—both human and otherwise—and cracked into the world. From a depth where all has grown mute and monotone, a question emerges: Why do people continue living in the presence of such monumental pain and suffering—in their own lives, those of dear ones, in the lives with only thin tethers to theirs. Memory lagoon, soft wash of words burst forth in the presence of a thing I am only just coming to understand. The shadows hiding in the angles of a sculpture or built structure or something amorphous: they regard you like a question, through side eye of stone and shade. You witness the impulse that another person had to become creator.

The darker spectrum of emotion produced by art and its practice calls to me. What is most overwhelming about confronting pain is that it is as singular as a wall that must be scaled. There is no way around it. Pain expresses itself clearly, as both a physical state and a mental one, towering above you, looking down upon you. Pain can be so severe that it overshadows all other senses and thoughts. Pain is like a place you go to by accident. When you arrive, you can't find the exit. Sometimes, in its worst moments, pain shuts out the possibility of properly observing other points of view and taking care of the world outside your head. It rears its nauseating crown in defiance.

Some people find pain to be romantic: nostalgia, bittersweetness, perhaps a memory you revisit to reshape it little by little, in the practice of artistic revision, until it becomes extraordinary. Unrecognizable if staged aside the irretrievable kernel itself. This kind of pain comes to you at an angle. Each year, one's accrual of experiences glosses the pain in magnifying layers, so that eventually you see through the part of the memory that burdens you like a refined telescope.

But true pain, the kind that makes you sick, is not redeemable in this way. An elusive substance. You simply cannot accrue too much of it before it turns you against yourself. Pain needs to be ejected; get it out. Even if it kills you. Remove the substanceless bile to clear your mind; a treacherous navigation with neither co-pilot nor direction. Journey meant to make alone.

Does darkness reach as extraordinarily far as suncast? Shadows are an exception to light, a respite in a desert and a pool of seductive relief in an otherwise garishly bright stretch of earth.

Self-expression is a risk. Though, when people turn away from feelings, they stifle what might be a profound delve into the porous limits of the human experience—a shunned chance to connect. Remind yourself that other people know pain. I like to imagine that we are more alike than not: artists remind us of this repetitiously. Artists are practiced in our ability to express ourselves. We have formed the tools (or have been given them) to say one thing in so many ways. When I write, I try to make one thing represent another, render a mood implicitly, unite oppositions, imagine a world that has been witnessed by no one. At times a vision perceived in the night room or one echoed to me from a voice I can't identify but which surely belongs to one of me. Perhaps I've not seen all I write with my own eyes. I approach the pain within and strangle it away. I circle it like prey before diving in to draw blood.

So many of us have something to say but imagine we do not have the outlet or time or knowledge: engaging with art, going to the museum for an hour, could be, in itself, a gesture toward artmaking. What you bring to the encounter is a lifetime. A work of art is what you understand it to be as your mind opens toward a person, allegory, culture, angle, hue, texture, sentence. You have a feeling about it and mustn't worry about whether someone will agree. Or perhaps you'll think about that later; it's good when people compare notes. Perhaps we create art in hopes that others will be moved by what they see to do the same.

Each chapter of this book displays an object, different things that I encountered over the course of writing this manuscript in order to interpret the pursuit of my own self-expression, because I have always related most to others through considering what song, color, or time of year makes them elated or distressed, frenzied or joyful. Some entities associated with the objects in this book are dear friends, one is a force of nature, some are strangers, a few are dead. Not all are lifelong favorites, nor do they indicate the particular aesthetic preferences of this writer. They are objects that have been created across thousands of years and continents of space; they reflect the districts of a journey. You'll see how arbitrarily I've come across most of these works of art.

What I find so rigid about "writing about art" is the institutional and structural pressure to check off scholarly marks, ones that need only apply to experts who intend to advance the field of art, at large, and the niches to which they devote their hard-earned knowledge. The past two decades have brought more abstract engagement between writers and the art they love. The most important part of the execution of the writing, to me, is to treat objects under consideration with dignity. Sometimes the objects conjure a memory. Perhaps they demand historical context. There are innumerable ways to approach art…it seems like I'm needing to remind myself of this constantly.

Pain takes the shape of a stone or a painting. Your interpretation of an object on a given day won't remain very long—indeed, the text within these pages breathe in and out of synchronicity with their creator. It will transform each time you wake, and inhabit repressed fantastical shapes while you sleep. It will grow meaningful to you and change you, like an old friend.

I must find the depths of pain, swim toward the bottom to know the intricacies of hurt and manifest myself in what I see to set the world ablaze. ✦

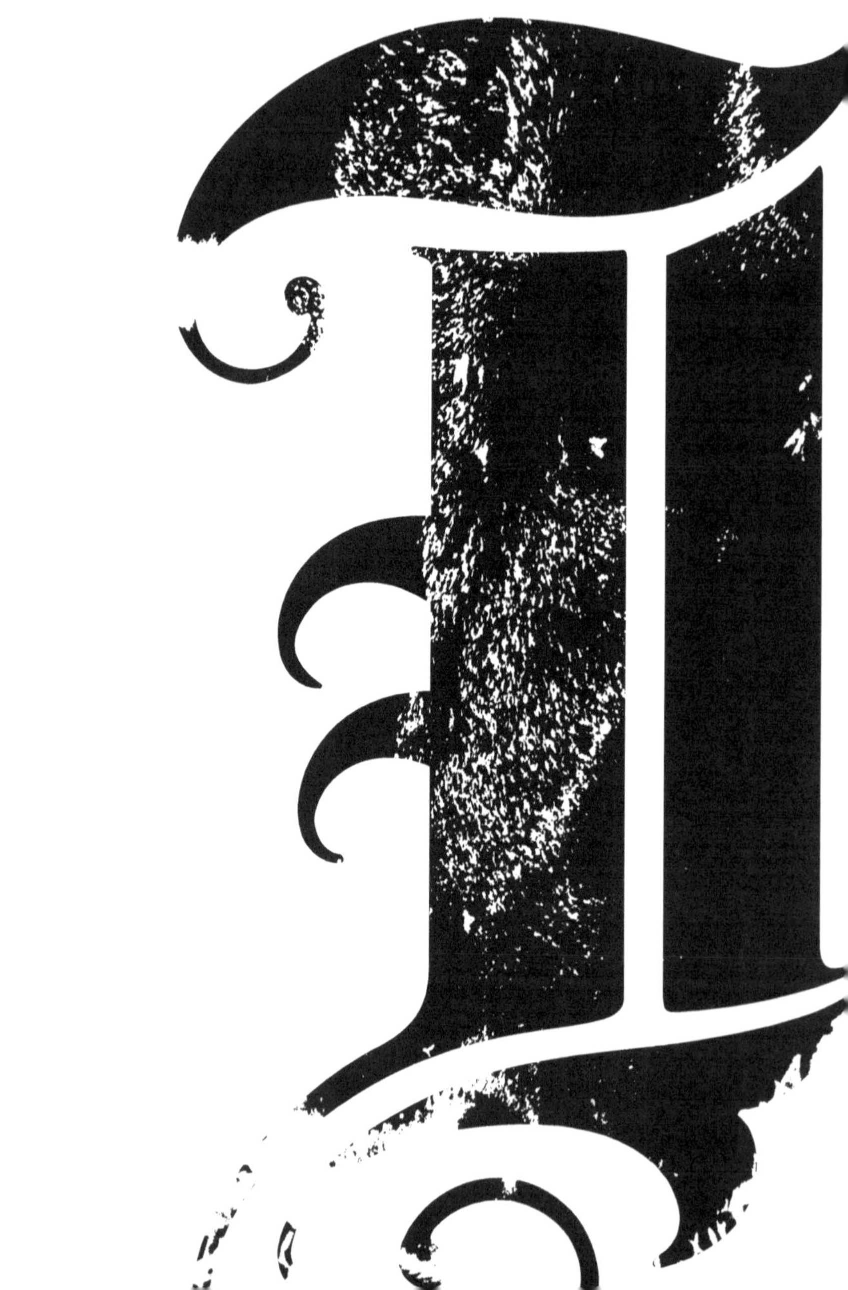

A S H E S

THROUGH THE ASHES I BEND. EVERY TIME I'VE TRIED to close my eyes to be consumed by blackness, out of nothing, the words begin. Once they start, I am unable to stop them, and even in moments visited by the soft absence of noise, they return. The words fill silence impulsively, a lonely ceaseless river.

I'm not sure of the meaning of the words, of what I'm hearing, but there is a heartbeat, an unchanging tone to them. It is a low tone of long serpentine ultraviolet waves. What I hear in my head is deeper than the frequency of my voice, and I wonder if the words originate from within me or if they come to me as an encrypted punishment. The words move with convicted velocity toward a frenzied surrogate dimension where decision is a trap door to an even more sorrowful level of the mind's labyrinthine catacombs. Where I am unarmed. My tongue tenses and curls into itself in shape of the words, attempting to form them inside the cave of my mouth where it is warm and where they are contained. I am purposeful in trying to end them so as not to be controlled. There are times the words cross the threshold of my lips, and I catch myself talking to myself, aware that now I'm speaking aloud, casting thoughts to nowhere. I wonder if the words take form in the physical realm. What are the repercussions? If they manifest, who do they reach? Does everything have a consequence in the seepage from the abstract into the real? Perhaps an imperial tempest rises over the dark Atlantic, garnering momentum as the words continue. I await the boiling storm.

xx   They are taking over. By the time I raise my eyes to my reflection in the mirror, I am unsurprised to see myself disappearing. Subtle fade of aura's glow, parts of the body are weaker than others and approach translucency. I ebb in and out. Strange specter. The words are so constant now that they form the landscapes through which I walk and think. I stumble over a dangling prefix, not sure of how each fragment and eventual sentence is supposed to end. It is only in purposefully listening to the words that I realize they course through my mind; my attention to them interrupts them. But as they grow acquainted to be-ing noticed, they resume their usual incantatory rhythm. The menial tasks of which my life is composed become but a backdrop for the words—too many words—passing through this mind. If they hope to entrench me, I'll unearth myself through exposing them.

And now, as I'm writing the words down, they become less clear than they were before leaving my head. My hand looks okay; it pushes the pen; it is the last remaining part of me to suggest that my body was once a more solid form. That I was once holdable. Trying to recall the words after witnessing them is a practice in memorization, not a practice in creation. I'm just reciting, like a part of the machine, laboring on in the penal colony. Fulfilling a pointless task to appease my own sanity. By the light of daybreak the words grow garish. To which of the senses do they belong? With their rise of hegemony this has become unclear. As they tumble from primal sound into signifier, they stretch into eleventh-dimensional shapes. The words can't stay, even as I write them here. How are we to express what we experience? I've never been able to get it right, always believing that what I wrote was unquestionably more beautiful than what I saw. Nothing I'd done had mattered. Before the words began, I had the increasing conviction that the moments from my life passed and were lost forever, falling apart and into a sticky pool of this girl's life. Each minute became untethered from the previous ones, until I looked upon me as a series of arbitrary fragments rather than as a journey neverending unto death. Memories lost their meaning and became distilled into clichés and clean endings. Everything could be explained away.

Even in the richest eminence hue of twilight hours, as the world envelopes its contents in the palette of slumber, the words whisper to me. I cross my arms over my chest and hope for sleep and stillness. But the words tell me stasis is a lie, that my dreams are a meaningless distraction from consciousness. What used to be sleep is an archangel of overwhelming restlessness, hours of laying at the mercy of the words. They keep me awake boundlessly through the night and into birds' chatter. The mourning dove's coo is no longer a gardenly comfort. When the sun crosses the horizon's threshold, I feel myself exposed. My pupils retract, disgusted by the arrival of another day, and I cower below the wet sheets in pursuit of a sleep that will not come. I fear the morning. Now how to live? All I can do is continue to lust for rest, craft a blanket of nostalgia for a time when it was silent.

The problem is that the words have started alienating me from the familiar people and places of daily life. In the city's noontime hours, I am moving through a world in which I once flourished, talking with beings and forms I know I knew, now guided by the words. On the street, the sound of my companion's voice loses its apexes and valleys, its rich death punctuated by a closing salty timbre, becoming some language I no longer understand spoken in slow and monochromatic syllables. I'm not sure what it is I'm supposed to be hearing. The outlines of her face and the rigid telephone pole behind her bleed into the gutter, stretching into indistinct oblong shapes pulled down by a gravity that refuses to ground me.

I know that it is the words who distort my senses, but I no longer perceive anything to be recognizably comforting. What's the point?

I wander off alone. I consume myself with the passing of time by looking at the clock; the slow unfurling, once-beauty of the progressing hours around me reminds me that I am not welcome here. Will this be my forever? I know that I am dying; I only wish it to come sooner.

I gaze to my feet when my head has grown wobbly in the absence of a sturdy neck; I've all but disappeared. I've gained some clairvoyance for the supernatural. Down below and much to my chagrin, I see myself, and beyond that, within the core of the Earth, all the variations of myself stare back at me. A cursed reflection—seeing too much—that allows me to try and pierce the walls of my ragged soul. In this reflection, roaches gnaw at my heels and chatter on my shoulders, glistening in the reflection of the sweat burning canyons into my neck. The words say I've paid no penance for moments of my life in which I failed to produce the desired result. I had wanted to be more. Punished for this terrible posture, the tendencies I could not control, for the woman I've been. There were innumerable times I separated from myself, acting out of a desire for liberation from my own constraints. Some parts I gave away in an anxious hope to become beloved, clawing for truth; I'd struck the tile with a red ball of fingers in my confinement and a vacant echo played on the other side of the wall; nothing much was left now. Had I known then what I'd feel now in the face of my current conundrum, I question if I'd have trodden more carefully, with calculation.

In a final act of defiance, I slough off the exhaustion. I close my eyes and imagine a way out of my subservience to the words. They have grown loud enough to mercilessly drown any other atmospheric sound. What I see around me and inside myself is now terrifying. The darkness I held sacred during my life has lost its seduction. There are no oceans to cross, so where do I come ashore? The beauty of our world is eradicated, as I am now beholden to the words. I cannot ignore what they have shown me about myself. I suspect the words know I plot against them, and they mystify me in entangling and inconceivable ways.

When I reach up to feel the sky or to caress the silver chain around the red spirit's neck, the words absorb the colors. Cerulean and metal, the phenomena of our world, snake toward my claws and into my veins, drawing in and dulling the vibrancy of my surroundings until all dims to a bordeaux so deep it blinds me. I am caught in a moribund spiral. The shriek that rises from within me is cast against the words. My remaining strength forms within my caving chest. It leaves my body with scorching fury, white hot. I am screaming.

My head hits the pavement. Its contents exit through a crack in the skull, and I feel the pressure release. Everything looks about the same from down here with my right eye to the old concrete. Snow piles silently around me. Sidewalk continues uninterrupted. Shoes tread past me, over me; I remain unseen. The sun and moon play in such quick, orchestrated succession that it appears as if someone closes and opens a spotlight up above. The words force me to retreat inside myself, and, from my womb, I suffocate on the blood that once sustained me, the life that was given to me in hopes that I would become a life of my own. I stop trying to breathe. I no longer perceive the space in which I move, reduced to just another death by asphyxiation.

The words have unraveled me, everything I loved. I am that which I fear, destroyer of all I touch. The acreage of my flesh is condemned: it's doomsday now. With no fantastical end.

++++++++++

There is nothing here in limbo but memory. I wrap my arms around my knees. The fact, I notice momentarily, is that I am not physically existing at all. I am just the projection of a sense, able to see without being seen, as I have finally, completely disappeared. Of course, I can't know for sure, but I surmise it. I'd felt looked down upon so often during my life, as I suppose everyone did in the privacy of her thoughts. I could never discern what role I was meant to play. That anxiety has dissolved now, and nothing but the space around me fills the space around me. It's not that I'm weightless—a force presses upon me. It is the force of all that to which I've bore witness and all that in which I've partaken. It cradles my carcassless being, peers down into my hazy presence. I cannot remember my life without my life regarding me. We peer into one another. The memories crowd together, a globe of unsteady rhythm...

My rainboots sink into the grass in a field full of bees, so full that I refuse to walk but instead cry until my mother picks me up, and the grey morning light slanting through my window is so bright that I know he has left me forever. I retreat into the circular crawlspace behind the tiny door as the figure of Moloch slinks around the house. In here it still smells of fresh paint and CD-ROMs. When I learned that he ate his wife's ashes in his cereal every day after she had been cremated, I built a memorial for myself in the forest, a place to bury—like Mathews said—the leaves at the bottom of a well. Depth was scarier than height, except for when the walls were too low. I saw the man lift the cigarette to his mouth and tumble backward over the viny ledge. This occurred in the quiet hours of the night. I gasped for breath and peered below to witness his body stretched on the pavement between the house and the parking lot. The library was just across the street. The lights within illuminated the snow with knowledge, introspection.

But, in a moment of distraction, the raven that landed on the banister was smoking a Marlboro red, like a cowboy. The dark lord of my dreams! Through corridors of Persian rugs I desperately searched for help, or even just an answer. I slammed my palms against the doors as I ran down the hall, but no one was anywhere. The one knob that turned opened to reveal a scene in which his mother held a shotgun to his dog's head. In another, the caretaker peered one-eyed through a crack, telling us not to come to the house again. We climbed over a fence in the backyard. Babble of a brook, evergreen petrichor, dark fire blistering through the night. I knew there was somewhere I was supposed to be going. I subsumed the pain of another that would last the rest of my life, and, upon my arrival at the mouth of the cave during avalanche season, I forgot the rest of the song. What key was it in, even? I continued pressing into the keys, quite arbitrarily as my fingers turned mossy, unsurprised to hear him telling me he'd be gone by la primavera. The ocean rose to meet me and into it tumbled each house on the cliff, where the white caps told of stormier weather and a whale expiring on the shore. His eyes saw mine as the ocean—so undividedly—in the neon smoke of the room that I started to cry. This wasn't my real hair. The liquid pooled beneath me on the bathroom floor. Cool winter air came in through the window; courtyard below of ruin and rat. Two days later, I stood to look out, of course I didn't mind the twisters forming on the horizon, because it never seemed they'd come near enough to destroy me. The few times I'd felt proximity, I'd inexplicably arrived at the eye of the storm. He didn't remember telling me that he loved me, and neither do I remember being loved. Avalanche season along the ring of fire. I heard the news. Where did you go, and why won't you answer me? Dogs choir next door barks to answer my head quietly against the wall of the tub. No loneliness in a city. I declined an invitation to the funeral, and got on the ship to cross the ocean before recalling I'd booked a flight. The ticket was stitched into the fabric of my left shin. One night I dreamt of a sickle, the next of a famine. No matter how many times I cast a line, the hook returned clean. Starvation became sus-tenance. I knew why the bruises on my knees refused to fade. I stopped healing. Thirty years passed. I whispered to myself that the pain would pass as a dewy petal returning to the earth in the shadow of a break in the trees. The terminating sky my palladium, in violet and garden and Cascadia. How is it that women never die?

All along. Everything important enough to keep. It wasn't clear to me then and it wouldn't be clear until years later, even after I had finished considering it, even now, as I consider it. I guess time and age distill what is important, cobbling together the images that compose a life.

Although sorrow shines brightly over memory, it comes from somewhere unreachable, like a glittering orb lodged in the sand of the chilly ocean floor. A sleepwalk drifted below every waking and unconscious act of my years—a part of my life formed outside of my control. It began quietly until it gained enough strength to voice itself, and thus began the words. They were born of regret, of longing, of self-loathing. I mistook my blue feelings as a side effect of human life. It grew within before radiating.

xxxPerhaps in my lifetime, the experience of womanhood was inextricable from an eclipsing nag of guilt. Girlhood as buffered by obsessive reflection, the quest to please, wide systems defined in the ego of the patriarchal code. I berated my own actions, believing I was poisonous. The responsibility was too great. I was torn between self-victimization and self-loathing, muscling entirely away from one and falling into the other, climbing out of the other and tripping into one. The words are the spawn of this internal warfare.

Like all writers, I located means of survival in reading; it unburdened me of the emotions in which I ensnared myself. There was one thing I did not realize until now, until after my own demise. The narratives of our world, regardless of the color of emotion or the breadth of intellect, all reveal how poorly we understand our role in the lives of others.

The course of my own life taught me one thing before this great fall: that we are owed love by no one.

A faint bell rings from far away, and the strands of earlier memory dissipate. Behemoth of great smoke carry away the wet fabric of me. My past becomes enigmatic to me, and I am returned to prehistory, bent into a knotted clutch.

My life was only something I caught whispers of in passing, like a sad story. Deep inside, an impenetrable scab has formed. I look for it, finding the gilded entrance to a tomb. When I lean against the door, I hear a faint twinkle, like the sound one thinks of upon seeing the gleam of one million platinum bars under a spotlight in an otherwise dark room. I retract in horror, but the little sound stays. A part of me has been taken away. ✦

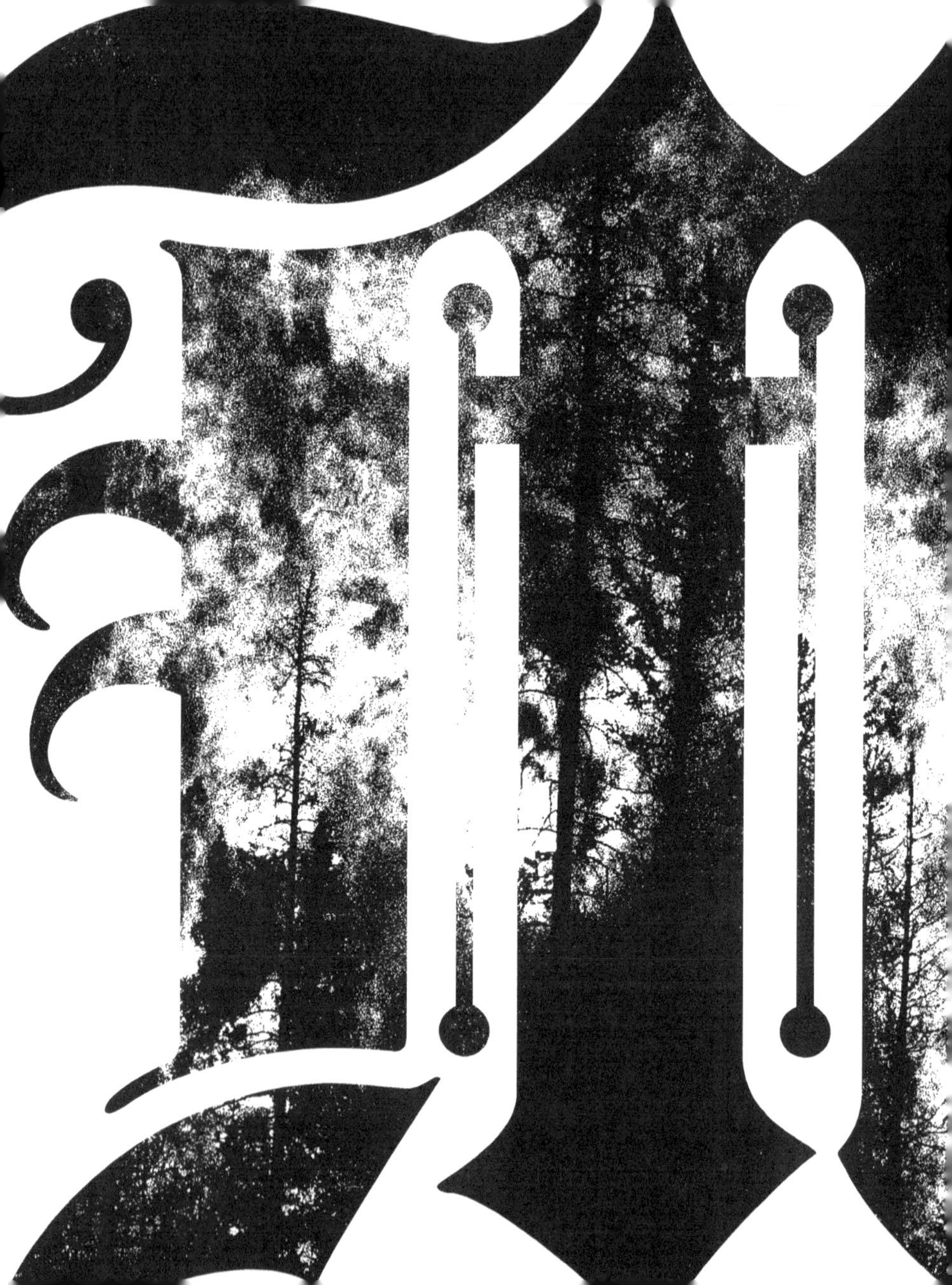

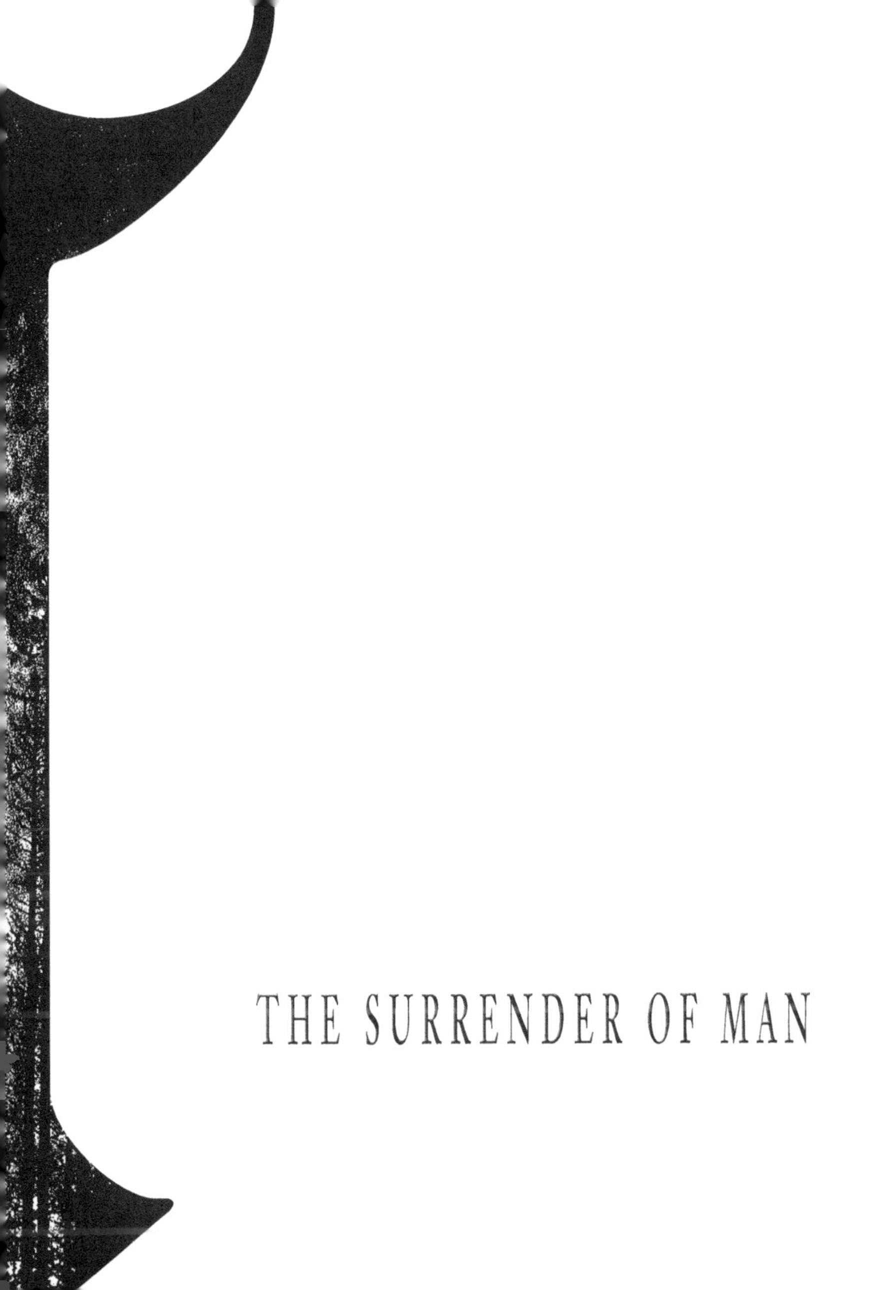

THE SURRENDER OF MAN

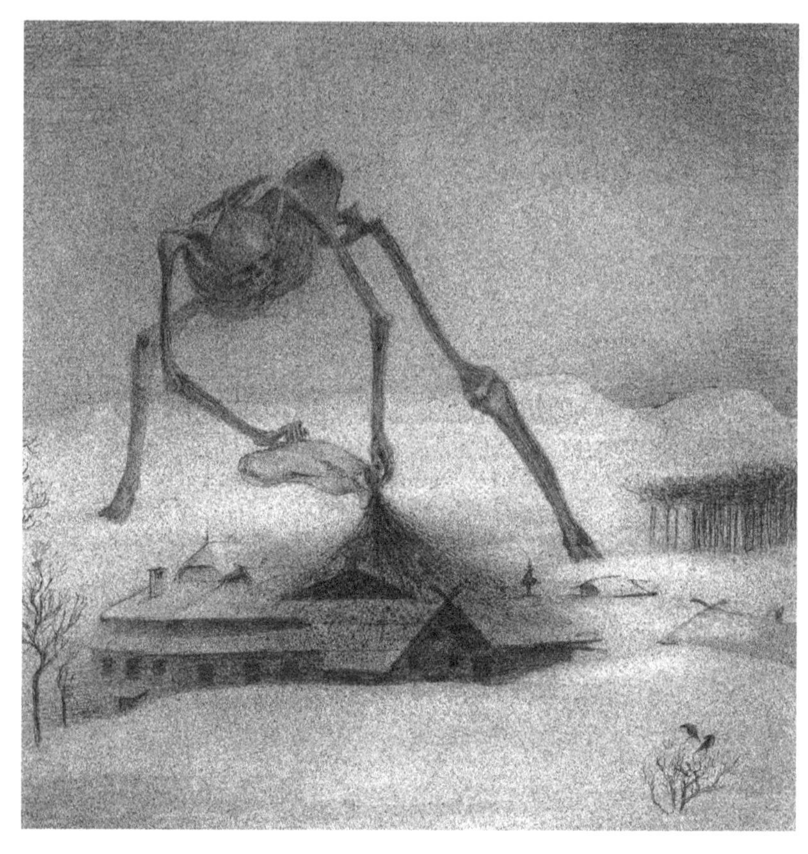

ALFRED KUBIN (AUSTRIAN, 1877–1959).
EPIDEMIE (EPIDEMIC), C. 1900–01. PEN AND INK
ON PAPER, 11 7/8 BY 11 ¾ IN. (30.3 X 30 CM).
MAX MORGENSTERN COLLECTION

CHAPTER 1

THE PERVASIVE ODOR OF DEATH CAME AS NO SURPRISE, craning its neck around corners in the city. I saw its thin hands reach from the cavern between gaping cellar doors as I walked down yawning avenues in the night. It fed me the words from a gleaming spoon.

I sought meaning from dark places, grasping for an explanation or a form of expression that might reveal life. The first time I saw Alfred Kubin's work—skeleton delivering an unmistakable death sentence—was on a twilight laptop Tumblr session in the early 2010s. At the time I was experiencing a significant pull toward mental escapism, dreaming of paths to waterfalls and fields of recurved tiger lilies. Of a jagged coastline. Most of the work presented on my Tumblr feed was contemporary and non-institutionalized: lots of fanart and representational portfolio paintings drawn after school. Perhaps the things I saw were well known in my community's realm but not in the circles that would eventually swaddle my life as someone immersed in the grasp of artspeak and its consequences as a young adult. The works were presented by the people who made them and shared by the people who followed them. During this slender window of Tumblr's history, it was harder to come across things you liked because there was less data harvesting and—at least in my experience—wildly nonexistent community guidelines.

I scrolled onto Kubin's drawing and screenshotted it for my photo files. It migrated from one device to the next over the years, until years later. I got a job at The Museum of Modern Art and I was surprised to find his works, via our online database, in our collection. I ended up contributing a short text about one of Kubin's drawings for the Museum's website, and only after it was published, I faced the fact that I knew nothing about him. I am pulled to write about him especially because he is relatively difficult to find out about. I think much of this has to do with how much of his later work was illustrative rather than standalone. He drew pictures to accompany other people's writings for decades of his life. I checked out one of his exhibition catalogues from the library, which I had under my jurisdiction for four years. *Alfred Kubin: Drawings 1897–1909* was compiled by Prestel and Neue Galerie to accompany the 2008 exhibition. Seeing as I'm neither an art historian nor someone who has spent years studying Kubin, I depend on this publication for most of my understanding of his work. As I was reading through it for the first time, I noted that Kubin was one of the few artists who had remained salient from my teens to my mid-twenties.

In *Epidemie*, pain comes without the possibility of respite. The artist's pencil strokes are quiet and intentionally placed in this work (not true of everything he did), trying so earnestly to be correct, as if in being executed properly the strokes reveal the unseen fabric of our world. This is what Kubin saw when he closed his eyes: death come to all. As pointed out in Prestel and Neue's catalogue, Kubin was drawing at the dawn of Freud's major works. Kubin "was not familiar with Freud's writing, and later rejected dream interpretation and psychoanalysis, with their subjective pathologies," but Freud's works "struck a nerve" at the time, nonetheless. Kubin's slim autobiography, which I viewed in NYPL's Art and Architecture collection, was written sporadically over the course of his life up until the year before his death. His thinking fixates heavily on ideas about psychological processes, and he tends to regard his own practice and output as an attempt to dissect.

The curious autobiography is punctuated with moments of poetic clarity. He writes, "One thing is certain, fantasy has put its hallmark on my existence, it is fantasy that makes me happy and makes me sad. I recognize it constantly inside and outside me." I can see this relationship to the fantastical manifest in *Epidemie*. Despite its messenger from beyond the grave, the composition doesn't feel totally fantastical; its kind of quietness—dampened, lonely, unfilled, as if in resistance—is delivered with great solemnity. In general, Kubin's work tends toward the macabre, conjuring images that disgust and frighten me. *Epidemie* feels comparatively muted, like his *Polar Bear* (1901–02). From whence has death arrived? On its own two feet, creaking over from one impenetrable tundra to the next. These barren landscapes are common for Kubin. The unspeakable occurs in places that have fallen out of time, indicated as Earthly only by a patch of foliage or the slope of a cliff into the sea. These places are abstract and in fact. And in both cases, Death takes the forefront.

I didn't know death as a child in that way that so many children live in permanent atrocity, but I was acquainted with it. Early memories seeped into my dreamscape and created a subconsciously spun eeriness that has faded over time. One of my earliest dreams was recurring, in which I found myself in a kitchenful of brass cookware so densely packed on all the shelves, even hanging from the ceilings, that it threw bronze light about the room, blinding me now and again. A noise from nearby kept catching my attention, a soft brushing of two pans. I'd search for the source of this sound over and over again, moving 'round the table in the middle of the room, unable to find it. As I approached the sound it would disappear and begin again across the room, under a cabinet. I grew accustomed to it, and it was not until the sound ceased that I knew something terrible had arrived. The silence of my solitude was then made apparent. The room was so orange. A silence that asked me to strangle myself; I was afraid to inhale. I couldn't envision the appearance of what was coming for me, but I knew it to be death. It would howl through the night.

I kept this dream a secret from my psychotherapist at the time because I knew that you cannot analyze away the definitive knowledge of death once it reveals itself. Death infects, it is never the infected; once you see it in your peripheral vision it is already too late, it cannot be unremembered. Life rearranges itself around the presence of death like children around the Maypole. America is, in particular, such a desperate onlooker of death. We cannot stop choking over the possibility that our healthcare

system, educational system, lack of housing, lack of support, police state, prison system, industrialized agricul-
ture, American-branded nihilism, might contribute to
the bloodlust. They say it must be the video games and
movies. Must be the art. We argue about wars waging
overseas of our own cause. Death lingers in certain corners here: the underground ones, the ones of marginal-
ized communities that the country refuses to see. The
ones who are afraid to walk alone at night or anywhere. I
see it out in Brooklyn. The trans girls. All girls. Anyone
without protection. Anyone feeling unwell. Death inflicts
from too many angles to identify. We love to be abstractly
shocked by death but when it confronts us, we cannot
make peace so instead tuck it away and underneath, never
within. We have been conditioned that any price is worthy to avoid being even death-adjacent. We could never
do right by someone who needed it the most.

Death crops up before me and reminds me of how little I
am prepared to handle it. One time I walked by a sullen
young boy in a red cloak on Fifth Avenue. He appeared
like an extra in a period film. As we passed one another,
he looked into my eyes with such penetration that I knew
him to be death. I caught myself unable to breathe. Death
has been a book with a note addressed to me under the

guise of love. It has presented itself on a rooftop at 8 a.m. as the sun broke horizon. It has branded me in three long strokes. It has crawled into the veins of my shifting body. Death was an unwashed sheet, folded on the dining table. It became more prevalent with onslaught of the words, shapeshifting from accent to centerpiece. Death was there at any formality; I walked around it.

I don't mean to say that I feared death. At times it came in peace, carrying away a life extended across decades. I accept endings as much as the next person. What I feared was experiencing death in the absence of all else. Like in the dream, seeing it overtake me in a moment of confusion. To die being unloved, not having made use of seasons through which I tumbled and turned.

Then death finally caressed me—its touch had no seduction, it impaled my chest—in the icy globe under a fluorescent evening, lulled by the smoothness of winter's heart. I saw myself sprawled before the black iron gate, sacrificed for nothing. Given to death as a gift.

When I'd first learned about Alfred Kubin, I'd been saddened by the onslaught of traumatizing circumstances of his childhood that carried him into adulthood—deaths in the family, his father's remarriage to his aunt, sexual abuse, feelings of solitude and isolation, an inability to (at first) fit in—and by the paltry documentation of his life that existed beyond his artwork. You have to imagine that images came to him as visions of fantastical torment. His drawings and paintings are a shriek amid silence, an answer if we ask what we see when we look for death: knives in place of arms and legs, hands clawing toward the surface of a black pool, marches into cavernous nothing and away from any recognizable universe. When people see his early work they say that it is scary, but I've not known anyone to dislike the work in light of that. As he grew older he sought other artistic pursuits and moved away from conversation with Death, despite his life's constant proximity to it. He moved toward, as he said, a "technical refinement."

The characters in these drawings made at the turn of the 20th century are not reaching out for you; they do not know you're there. An idea unfolds before your eyes. The works are so darkly imaginative that your impulse is to begin drawing a story around them. You witness them and withdraw into yourself, grow lonelier so that you may rest in horror's gray embrace. Kubin let himself dwell in it: he staked claim in the agony of fear. ✦

✦ ✦ ✦ ✦ ✦ ✦ ✦ ✦ ✦

THE PULSING OF MY BRAIN AGAINST MY SKULL HAS A definitive rhythm which distracts me from getting back into the day. Later on, I feel the water on the slimy tiles grow colder; it rains down from above not a punisher but a directive; catalyze the watering and flood the seedling; impermanence of temperature; the actual experience from outside itself cannot be retold. I have as little an idea of what is happening as you. The great command arrives from the green pipes and is wasted on my uncontained body. I'd never really wondered—or cared—about its source. Water is ephemeral and unpredictable.

I feel compelled by unbridled waters, ones into which I might dive or cast. How they roll in marine and tumble in sprays of white on a rainy day. Lullaby of the deep. When I was a kid I thought it was the downpour of the sky that kept the ocean filled. And doesn't it make sense? The dreams of water I'd often try to record and regurgitate in my work when I first began writing prose so many years ago. The writing always felt too clever, too contrived. Forcing the reader to devise complex associations based off thinly drawn metaphors and images that were better left in the slippery domain of my own subconscious, not to be bothered.

I swam in an ocean surrounded by a field of jellies; saw a late friend perched atop his own memorial above a shallow pool; trudged along a cliff as the water arched over my head, never tumbling upon me. Things to me that held a mystery, a great hope. Perhaps I grow further from the search for wonder as years pass me, depending less on reactions to experiences—especially ones that were new and horrifying at more tender ages—to perceive a veritable truth that the world keeps going with or without me.

I think that my life began with a dream I can't remember. I'm only chasing what I can't remember. A series of images I'd witnessed before I had the capacity to shape memory into a story, before I knew better than to believe in the promise of life. ✦

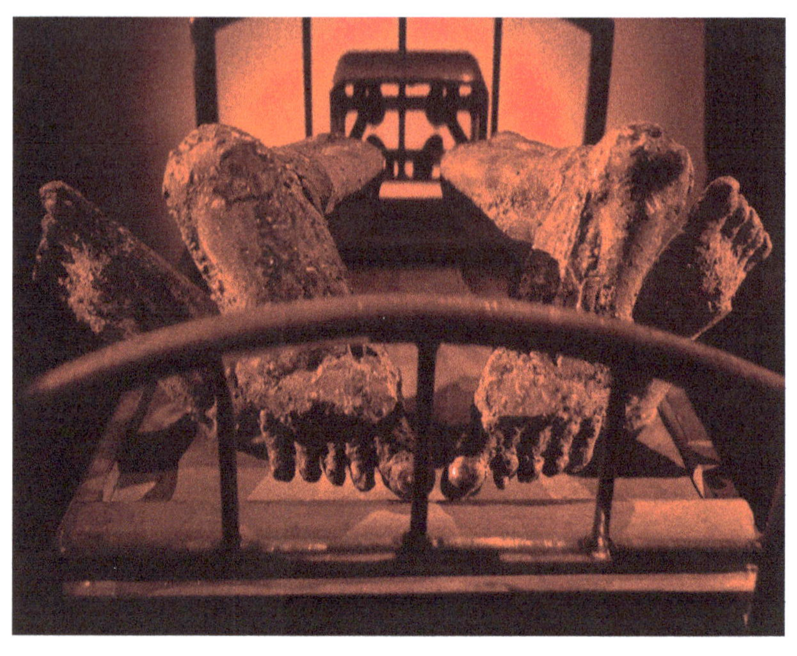

CHAPTER 2

I COMPLAIN THAT WRITERS OF MUCH EARLIER decades had the luxury of time: to walk, to sit, to contemplate. When I imagine their days, they seem unbelievably bronzed, slowly turning, wine afternoons and reverberatory solitude—consumed by less desperation than mine, perhaps. Knowing less of everything at once. Information more a pursuit and less a thin (but miraculous) fabric. A life of a different color, an antiquated form of sunrise to sunset that cannot be reconciled with our twenty-first century, the long scroll. My commuting for three hours a day, eating bodega dinner on the train while copyediting a poem. Goes without saying that its easier to be lulled to submission in the predictable structure. It's hard to get out. Burnout and meaningless appeal to the corporate realm. Devotion to a job that's supposed to get you somewhere. When I was committed to noise, I didn't follow the wanderings of my brain but instead let them ripple beneath the surface of my skin. Life seems to have happened so quickly, in a bright flash. But, in concept, death is infinite. From a quiet and still place it occurs to me that what I'd wanted so desperately in life—time to think, clarity of thought—is now available to me, as writing bends time and structure and the hours stretch out before me, are moving away from me.

In some museums, the presence of works of art are birthed and overlapping like the shapes through a kaleidoscope. Works arrive on loan, briefly entering the Museum's offerings before being shipped home (or to the clutches of their captors). Some collection works can be found on display like old friends, others appear unexpectedly, brought out of storage for periods of time to star in an exhibition or to be studied or undergo a check-up. The unexpected nature of spotting an art object that caresses you into the shadowy, forgotten corners of your mind is something I cherish about the frequency through which I walk through the galleries of The Museum of Modern Art, where I worked.

I encountered a series of eight holograms by Louise Bourgeois at 2019's *New Order: Art and Technology in the Twenty-First Century*, curated by Michelle Kuo with Lina Kavaliunas. The exhibition was in the second floor galleries off the Atrium with high ceilings and meadows of space. The rooms were severe sleek with black accent walls. Each time I revisited Bourgeois's work, I watched museumgoers shuffle forward and backward to experience the optical illusion of this strange and unexpected suite of works.

The first time I encountered the untitled hologram series I was surprised. It seems quite anomalous within her oeuvre because of its dependency during production on new media (lasers). And although produced by machine, the series was arguably liberated from its technologized dependence the minute the works were completed. Just add light. The finished pieces are filmlike in their viewer-activated mimicking of motion. But her subject-matter looks ancient. The edges of the portrayed objects are rough with time. You can see it in the crumbling of the parts of bodies Bourgeois chooses to signify.

The affective part of the work is that your own movement heightens the stagnancy of what is portrayed. Repositioning yourself from left to right in front of it provides an extremely limited change in perspective—maybe an inch shift of the hologram—so no new compositional elements are introduced by the viewer's movement. I am constantly hoping for agency to improve my line of vision. It does not occur and leaves me feeling frustrated, as in a dream when everything is just too bright. The provocation for seeking agency without the ability to achieve agency. Unlike Alfred Kubin, Bourgeois's own practice was directly positioned in respect to Freudian psychoanalytics (Jewish Museum's recent 2021 exhibition was entitled *Louise Bourgeois: Freud's Daughter*).

The obscured view Bourgeois provides leaves the question: what exactly are you meant to be seeing? Two pairs of feet, connected to rods, connected to a jailbar bedframe. In this particular hologram, your view is too level with and close to the scene to grasp context. Bourgeois has only supplied a crude suggestion of humanity.

In its darker moments Bourgeois's work can grow personal and remind me of being enchained in a relationship where hegemonic structures do not play in your favor, of being constantly forced to face something you seek to flee. Thus an element of fear is introduced. The pairs of feet are arranged in a suggestion of intimacy, as if one person lays atop another. But this arrangement is suffocating and forceful. Another note of investigation finds desperation, as if proximity is for survival rather than pleasure or fulfillment. An even darker interpretation travels darker roads; reads force, manipulation, rape. The textures of the feet appear abject and crusty: fleshly decay or a primitive cobbling together of material to create the impression of a body or of humanity once inhabited.

We tend to be horrified by that which resides in the uncanny valley, by anything similar to us that lacks our capacity to emote. When we try to look into the eyes of a piece of artificial intelligence, we find the blankness disturbing. It's not doing what we want it to do; it's giving us nothing and does not have the capacity to care about our humanity. Those cursed AI edits permeating the Web (Balenciaga Harry Potter) where the only movement of a human figure is the brief tilt of a head, lock of hair moved by wind, hand shifting aside the hip. Bourgeois's mechanical suggestion-imitation of corporeality disgusts me in a similar way. It mimics the human experience in form, chaining it to infinite immobility. I can't fully make sense of what Bourgeois has depicted no matter how closely I consider it, but I know that the entire bleak world is contained within the hologram. I cannot see six walls around the bed, but I know that they stand erect and that nothing lay beyond them. Stuck here, like me. But one other thing: the words have stopped. When I look inward, I find silence waiting to be filled. My mind is my kingdom, and although it is populated with dark and isolated ideas, each one produces a correlating image. I'm not sure this has ever been my experience of the world. I can now see what I think. I have regained my imaginative capacity. The words no longer override my own attempt to make a thought. ✦

In another dream of mine, I stooped over a sink filling with water. When it reached the brim, the faucet remained on but did not cause the sink to overfill. Uncomfortable stagnancy infinity of the subconscious. This image kept invading my thoughts in the weeks that followed. Though it seems obvious now, it took me awhile to extract that what I despised about the dream was that something so elemental had acted unexpectedly.

See, in dreams, as with art, I've found that I have to come at something from a parallel angle rather than approaching it directly. It is not the image itself of defied physical law that overwhelms me, but the possibility that something extraordinary could occur and that I would be unable to understand it as it unfolded before my own eyes. ✦

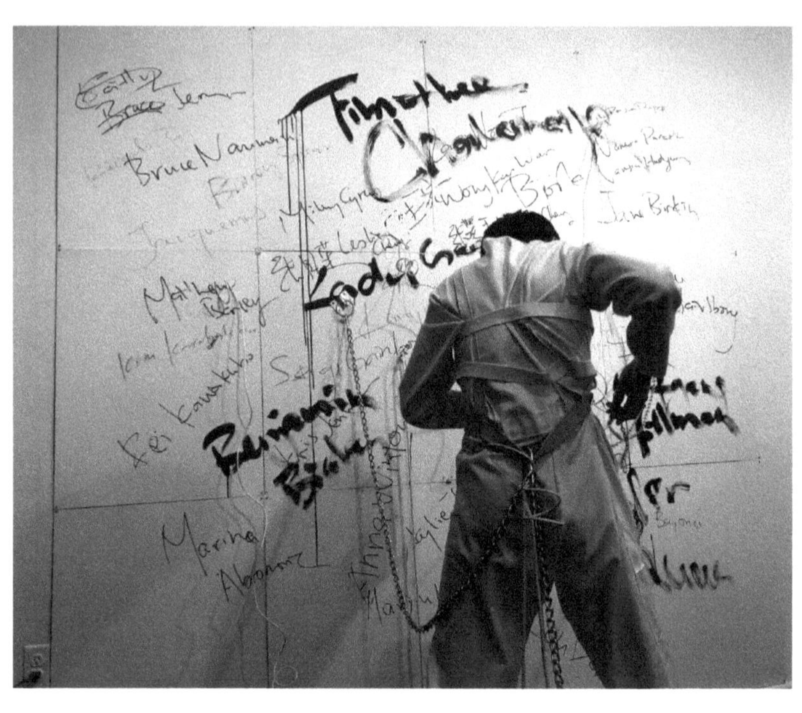

ALEXANDER SI. ATLAS. 2020. GRAPHITE,
ELECTRONIC CABLES, HARDWARE, STUDS,
DRYWALL. DIMENSIONS VARIABLE.
PHOTO COURTESY THE ARTIST

CHAPTER 3

"Like Atlas who was punished to shoulder the
weight of the world, a modern spectator is
tied down by their own mind map, an imagination informed by the superabundant media
culture."

— ALEXANDER SI

SOMETIMES WHEN I USED TO SIT DOWN TO DRAFT
out a piece of prose, I made a deliberate effort to copy and
paste the text messages that arrived, that I read while writing, into the work as I went along. It seemed more hon-
est than trying to convince any reader that my attention
was only focused on and influenced by my own invention.
No other generation of writer had been inundated with
disembodied—but verifiably real—other people and their
thoughts and feelings during the writing process in this
way. Felt special, cursed, fresh.

My focus is as shot as the next Millennial's. My thinking spills into crevices and beyond my own reach; grows unattainable and lost; images appear arbitrarily in my mind (I just saw a train, for example); why can't the work be manic if it is to be true? There is no need to suggest pure meditation. I speak from within my condition. I "love" machines because I like to think that I have so little in common with them. I am interested in the singularity because I want to know what I would be like if I were more precise, less porous, less pathetic. The gaps in my mind and body give entrance to phantoms; in one of my infinite parallel universes I guard myself by pouring cement into every crevice, a keep, finality in assurance. I'm not pitying myself, I just believe knowing where your mind is at is part of the human journey.

One time I sat with Alexander Si at his studio. Outside the sky poured over Manhattan's Chelsea and we talked about *Glitch Feminism* and the art industry and the hot topics of early 2021. We loved to gossip. He showed me artifacts of various recent projects and scrolled through renderings of a forthcoming exhibition, exhibiting his multimedia expertise with a critical deftness I've always cherished. His work tackles so many things: the Britney Spears legacy, contemporary fast-salad chains, self-help, social media use, and the widespread social problems that arise from all of these. At the time, he operated a gallery, 24 E Broadway, autonomously while also working full time. This willingness to both take up and create space is part of what's made New York's non-elite/emerging/indie/whatever art scenes feasible during my time here. As Si speaks, his mind is a vessel that distills large abstract concepts into shrewd contemporary discourse. I always leave our conversations with a lot on my mind, feeling inspired to tackle my own creative borders. As we said our goodbyes that afternoon, he offered me a piece of his installation *Atlas*, a work that had existed in several iterations over a span of two years. A few weeks later he'd come over to install it in my Brooklyn apartment, over the river and train rides away.

Alexander Si makes a map. He releases names in his head automatically, scrawling them onto a wall with vehemence, his wrist like stone: Bruce Nauman, Lana Del Rey, Serge Gainsbourg, Leonard Cohen, Lou Doillon, Abel Tesfaye, Kim Kardashian. The names that occur to him are those of big presences: models, filmmakers, celebrities, writers, musicians, artists. They reveal that perhaps, on this given day, the artist had a certain sensibility for the threads of glamour and fame that gloss human history. To have your name remembered by a loved one is one thing; to have it remembered globally and timelessly is another. It is hard to imagine never being forgotten. Quite horrifying to imagine that your name will tumble through time uncontrollably and perhaps take on unexpected meaning in the centuries to come. To lose grip of your story. This grid of names: a dazzling and blinding map of the blue Earth, or an accumulation of a particular mind's knowledge. When you look at it from afar the names appear rigid, contained, and entombed. Close up, his handwriting is rushed without being sloppy; lines are over or underextended and stylized. There are different weights to the text depending on which writing utensil the artist has used: a pencil, a pen, a thick marker.

Eventually Si covers the grid. He crucifies the names with various fasteners, connecting them associatively using different ropes and strings attached to his back. Who has worked with whom? Who is related to whom? Related in what way? Whose secret crimes tether them to another of these elite rulers? He grows entwined to the names which have only just passed through his mind. There are consequences to thought. What you let occur to you might burden you forever.

I suppose all maps hold a promise of finality, whether or not the map be just or evil, held in common belief or devised to invade and rule. I wonder if those early cartographers imagined how their shapes of the Earth's surface would change, by force of both human precision and human damage. What they have in common with Si's map is an attempt to make one thing stand for another. Artfulness… When I was young and had to draw an outline of a country or a state, I would shake my hand lightly to mimic the jagged coastal lines on maps of the world; there was no perception of the lines denoting a finite space, a navigable space. In the artist's case: this "mind map" (as Si puts it) signifies the saturation of popular culture in everyday life. His brain is steeped in it: unboxing videos, YouTube feuds, on-and-off again Instagram, watching every film ever featuring a particular actor, being unable to pull oneself away from the screen at night until realizing the sun has risen. The fear of what happens when you sleep too close to your phone. The fear of being away from the phone for too long and the knowledge that life will creep on behind ones back. It's a kind of mania that is so routine for so many of us that it has become banal. We joke about our lack of mental hygiene and meltdowns, our sh*tposting and our psych ward visits, our prescriptions and our insomnia. We are as unable to escape the grid as the names on the *Atlas* wall. We block celebrities on social media to avoid their ghoulish manifestation in our lives but they reappear on different channels, selling us some product or representing some cause.

As part of Alexander's performance, he turns away from his map and attempts to yank the work from the wall in heavy gestures. The performance becomes a labor of destruction; the manual demolition of work and representation; a literal removal of what ties the artist down. Some of the chains break free from the wall. Some of the panels fall off in chunks. Tatters of it drag behind him on the floor.

There is delight in seeing Si destroy his work with a fully developed yet controlled rage, leaving behind only the ruins. The viewers of the month-long exhibition see the tattered wall and can only reconstruct the original in their imaginations. Post-apocalypse of an artist's mind, the viewer left with a quiet detritus. All of Si's work is heady, though not purely conceptual. He loves appropriating the spooky sleekness of Big Tech's designs. He introduces himself to you on the ocean's surface before dragging you into density and darkness, where you will learn to light your own way and discover species unknown. ✦

✦ ✦ ✦ ✦ ✦ ✦ ✦ ✦ ✦

IN WRITING WE OFTEN DISCUSS THE "SUSPENSION OF disbelief," which is the idea that, at times, we should set aside our skepticism in exchange for our full immersion in a story or experience. This practice was one that I frequently enacted as I grew older. I became an atheist at a young age (if I remember correctly, I was nine) and felt a constant frustration that my non-belief was offensive to my god-fearing friends, when in my reality, I felt I had more reason to be offended by their worship and by the history of exploitation and abuse that outlined religion across the globe. Earlier on I, unfortunately, had barely any tolerance for other people's notions of belief.

I did not seek counterarguments to the possibility of the existence of god, but I did wish for evidence of god's existence. None surfaced, and as the years went on and I learned about existentialism and gave language to my godless visions, the random nature of life became increasingly startling. ✦

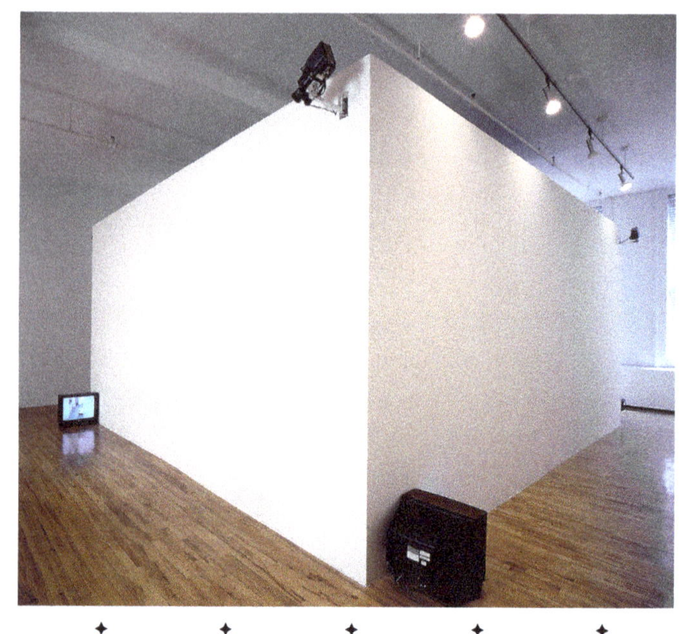

Bruce Nauman. *Going Around the Corner Piece.* 1970. Closed-circuit video installation, four black-and-white video cameras, four black-and-white monitors, wallboard, paint, 10 x 20 x 20 ft. (304.8 x 609.6 x 609.6 cm). Musée national d'art modern, Centre Pompidou, Paris. Acquisition

CHAPTER 4

MY EXPERIENCES HAVE TAUGHT ME THAT IT'S POSSI-
ble to think my way out of a corner, a necessary coping
mechanism if you want to see more years. Small things
shock the system out of stagnancy. Sometimes I think
about how the language of rehabilitation facilities or
mental health wards can be dogmatic but I have found
it to be true that no one can help you until you help
yourself. If you want to water a flower you need to tilt
the can towards the earth. Etcetera, you've got to know
when you're stuck.

Some works of art provide resolution and harmony. They
have colors that soothe you, or perhaps the artist moves
their brush with a technical mastery that replicates a fold
of skin or the infinite pool of the surface of a human eye.
Proximity to "reality" could be a very early form of appre-
ciation for art because it is so obvious; anyone with seeing
ability can judge if a work reminds them of what they see
beyond the canvas. This is art that hypothetically appeals

to a god's or creator's intentions (obviously in the case of European Renaissance, this lifelikeness of skin was seductive to the wealthy patrons, essentially gods, who ordered the work to be created). While some of the work whose value could be heavily rendered via theory feel a bit unkind, other works of art render you a mouse under the command of a playful feline. They force you to weave through labyrinthine thoughts with or without extensive art historical knowledge. In the confounding process of finding out what the artwork means to you, you realize you've forgotten what it was that had bothered you earlier that day.

I'd made initial contact with Bruce Nauman's work in the basement of sweeping Dia Beacon outside New York City. I'd never been there before, as I was still somewhat new to the city. Compared to the heavenly washes of space in the upstairs gallery, the basement acted like a complementary underworld. It was barely lit, and I wandered through a body of work that drew me in for its off-putting and masochistic qualities. Sometimes, installations can present immediate shock that later fades: a body of work could be highly experiential or be notable for cheap shock-value (I think of those turn-of-the-2020s atrocious "art" shows around the empty floors of buildings in Manhattan and other major metropolises that provide an experience for photo-taking rather than an experience of art and financially benefit no one who needs it—well-meaning people spend generous wads of cash to see these exhibitions where the artist's [public domain] work is cheaply projected around some ex-WeWork office space organized by "Exhibition Hub," funded by the likes of Goldman fucking Sachs. Really divorcing the meaning of "curation" from any recognizable iteration of the word's meaning. It's masterful grifting with money well-spent for whatever sicko investors plastered ads for these "experiences" on everyone's Internet and billboard. At least museums plaster the names of their demon funders on the names of their galleries without trying to hide it…).

I knew Nauman immediately to be my kin, to be someone whose ideas would stick around and become influential to my own. At Dia, there's the famous *Hanged Man* (1985), in which a neon sculpture flashes once to show a stick figure with an exaggerated flaccid penis and twice to show the same figure, asphyxiated, and hard. The masculine body is at once a source of comedy and tragedy. It is depicted as pitiful but relatable. Another work on view, entitled *South American Circle* (1981), suspends a sideways chair inside a metal ring slightly above the viewer's head, casting graveyard shadows that entrap you. Nauman's body of work is oftentimes praised for its incorporation of multitudinous forms and ideas: I'm thinking of his cages, his fountains, his tragic clowns on tape. He kind of just does whatever. But when I encounter him, I indulge the angular feeling his work evokes. Its eeriness is pornographic, gives you the creepy crawlies.

I appreciate him because he's a freak, not in spite of it. When Nauman's retrospective was being installed at MoMA in 2018, I was still an intern. I distinctly remember how much I started sweating as I lugged the advance copies of the Nauman catalogue around the Museum for the senior management who are always graced with the earliest copies of our publications to arrive from the bindery. I was new to this job and generally confused about how to get to the various offices and I didn't manage to look at the cover of the book until I handed the first copy to its recipient. I was shocked that I hadn't realized we were about to showcase such a large body of Nauman's work, but at the time I was still learning the flowcharts and processes and intricacies of life in a new (corporate-ish) atmosphere.

One of the best parts of working at a Museum is getting to see the art outside normal hours of operation. When I finally made it to see a preview of the exhibition in MoMA's airy sixth-floor galleries (a large part of it extended to PS1), I was delighted. In Nauman's *Going Around the Corner Piece* (1970), the top corners of a closed-off square room are flagged by surveillance cameras. At the end of each side of the wall sits a television monitor showing a closed-circuit feed. As I approached the installation, I looked down and expected to see my tiny, pixelated replica displayed on the screen. But no one was there, and it took a moment to understand that each monitor is, in fact, displaying the activity *Around the Corner*. Like *Hanged Man*: broad social commentaries with an edge that's a little bit funny, little bit snarky. I took a photo with my phone to remind myself how much I liked the work (October 17, 2018, via Instagram archive).

Nauman has a fixation on closed-circuit feeds of this nature. I'm thinking of *Audio-Video Underground Chamber* (1972–74) which is a feed of an empty underground chamber that no one can access. He plays with a viewer's expectation, not showing you what you anticipate seeing, withholding information (like Bourgeois's holograms), breaching your privacy, frustrating you. The work is beautifully cruel. It won't explain itself to you. *Going Around the Corner* is unsolvable. Fucked up games like this remind me of when I watched the exquisite *Saw II* with a bunch of older teenagers when I was younger. Whether or not I enjoyed it, it left an impression. Liking things can be a trauma response! I think about this movie all the time; it is like an intrusive thought. At the time, I was intrigued by why someone would produce such gore in pursuit of art; life of a child before saturation in film theory and various avenues of media literacy training. Over the years I'd watch the rest of the franchise and eventually emphasize horror film theory in academic pursuits. It is unsurprising that my affinity for visual art tends to lean into the cynical, spooky, and dark given the loud memories I have of witnessing horror film over the years. Hard to define the attraction of a child to what moves them.

While walking around the four walls of *Going Around the Corner Piece*, the viewer chases her own image, attempting to catch herself under surveillance. Her behavior is broadcasted only beyond her reach for others—or no one—to see. Some hazy silver specter lost without the company of another to suggest *she was there*. Like 1980s storefronts filled with televisions in the twilight flashing unwitnessed. It's an uncontrollable failure of communication, a system stacked against you. A useless technology. I find it pleasurable to encounter feelings of frustration in attempting to engage with an artwork that refuses to give you what you want; an abstract unfulfillment; a fetishized scolding. And I am certainly not unique in this sense. For the artist is a household name, In the world of visual art, Bruce Nauman has achieved it all.

In the broader public arena of the written word, so many narratives we feed each other have a trajectory with a beginning, a climax, a conclusion (This book? That's for you to decide.). Popular culture proves nothing if not our increasing and unquenchable thirst for excitement and projection into adventure. To our credit; some popular culture is contrived à la backend deals like the dreaded industry plant or US Army-backed movies that liberal arts college film bros pseudointellectually theorize into oblivion. But some works we popularize on our own, especially within the literary world. And so many of these narratives never made sense to me. Look at the *New York Times* bestsellers, even the institutional award-winners. Even the most passionate and masterfully-written memoirs of redemption read too cleanly: they arrive to us packaged, preplanned, bursting at the seams with their eagerness to transition where they're supposed to and hide loose threads within quaint narrative details of a upward-swinging life. *People are looking for a good story* is what you're told when you begin to study writing within an institutional framework.

Are "people" so bovine? People don't always need a life-line. How alienating to look at the stories around you and feel that none relay a reality you recognize or share; you can fixate upon fringe material (BDSM) without normalizing it (*Fifty Shades*) or discuss issues of race (in America) without perpetrating the problem (reposting the same infographic seen by millions, for example, in lieu of more actionable ways to directly support Black people, or, more recently, Palestinians via the "All Eyes on Gaza" AI graphic). This frustration is meant to be felt together, you and me.

I thirst for art that can't be encapsulated by even the most expansive review or a description. I could never retell the stories that the artists in these pages express because the work they produce could only ever have come from *them*. When I try to distill the elements that compose their work, the unified liquid bursts into this extended love poem you are reading. Nauman is institutional to be sure, but his work still makes me delight in its constraining architectures and dark clown humor. It disregards this impulse toward comfort or toward teaching a moral lesson. It shows how seriously he regards other people's capacities to think. It makes me want to look around and it makes me want to read. It moves me to choose humanity even in moments where our atrocities bend me toward a yearning for solitude. He wants me to bite off *and* chew. I play ball, involving myself in his mind games. I am compromising with the work he presents, not following it. Locating myself within it. I'm encountering it and expecting to see myself reflected in it and instead, see nothing. ✦

✦   ✦   ✦   ✦   ✦   ✦   ✦   ✦   ✦

THE EXPERIENCE OF WITNESSING ART ENTANGLES ME in a fevered journey through the landscape of my own mind. It must be similar to the experience of religion, in that you are oftentimes drawn into understanding through a journey of emotional change. I like art that squirms in the realm of darkness. Intrusive and disturbing elements and images are confrontational by nature and coax me into the far edges of my emotional spectrum. I feel intoxicated by artists who show me something that shocks me. Perhaps because the world I know is weighted with inconsolable agonies which move me toward the practice of all of this (writing, art criticism, waxing poetic to a fault).

Years ago, on a winter evening above the crowded bar, in a railroad apartment doubling as artist studio, I wept before a set of paintings, in prayer, in recognition, of this construction by an artist of tormented figures who over and over again reminded myself of me. Slippage between reality and representation is a dangerous place. Pursuit of art and its witnessing wringing me out like an enemy's revelations. Cusp of art and life no longer present, collapse of border into salty brine. Brain like boat in bottle. Between whispers of memories and immediate sensory stimulation, and all the bodily capabilities I'd lost during the surrender of man return to me. ✦

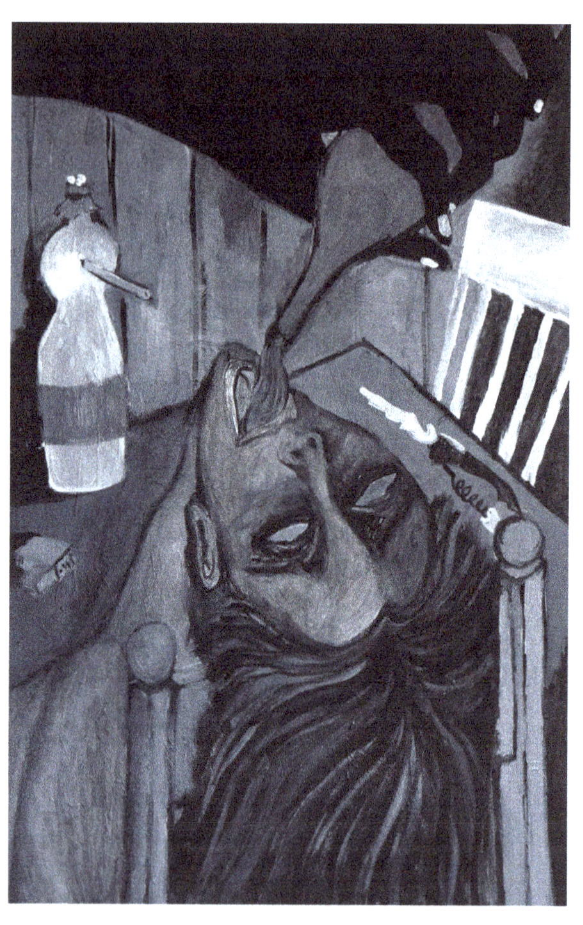

Elia Bianchini. *Untitled*. 2019. Oil on canvas. 36 x 24 in. (91.5 x 60.1 cm). Gift of the artist

CHAPTER 5

THE YOUNG ITALIAN PAINTER AND TATTOO ARTIST Elia Bianchini, was living in Brooklyn at the time, busy making work and waiting tables, being cool and social. I'd met him in the k-holeic basement of some experimental musician friends when I was playing photographer for the night. His practice was primarily based in tattoo but he was beginning to paint more seriously, and his work bled sadness. He loved Modigliani. His characters were of an earlier time. They held knives, flowers, the hands of their dance partners; they journeyed and lamented a loss of love or life. They were people perpetually blanketed in nightfall. When Mina Hamedi and I started an independent goth art magazine entitled NAUSIKÂE, Bianchini was one of the first contributing artists to come to mind. He exceeded our expectations for the inaugural installment of the magazine and executed a series of nine grayscale paintings, oil on canvas, despite how he'd recently leaned towards acrylic. He invited me to see them in the middle of a light evening snowfall that made the world feel ancient.

In the series, the palpable world slips away from its inhabitants as a faceless omniscient intruder takes the stage: coercing them with the sinful engagement of carnality and drugs and the ultimate escape. In certain encounters, this godlike figure commits dirty deeds with the inhabitants of Bianchini's world. Images of sexual pleasure aren't liberating; they're vacant. No desire is filled. This is not Hokusai's *Fisherman's Wife*.

In my favorite of the paintings, the woman's eyes appear empty at first, though they accrue power and upon second glance they cut through the painting. They are introduced to a murky light from the outside, ready to obey or be inhabited. There is abandonment and ecstasy in the limp craning of the neck over the back of the chair. The hand or pair of hands that appear in most of these paintings always slinking in from an unknown part of the room: the puppet master. I suspect otherworldliness. Down the woman's throat slips a smooth and plunging liquid promise: escape and ending. The viewer watches the orchestration of the downfall and is thus made a helpless perpetrator. Who brings narrative to a painting if it is not witnessed? In being viewed the work is brought to life.

The person in this painting is forced by her ruler to become a feverish oracle, to act and speak on behalf of the down below. What roads had she crawled to meet this eternal damnation? In the absence of agency, she was a vessel for the influence of, oh, anything. I looked into a mirror, a doll's house. An image of a globe of Earth whipped through a lick of fire. Chaos unleashes in the event that humans witness a new dimension. How can you grasp something you can't quite perceive? Not sure if I am writing or if this is being written. I hope you understand. I've heard of it; it happens now, I think. Blue spirals into soot, a fury of selves unleash into me. They shred through the spaces in my ribcages. Each passage through the body pronounces a discordant bitonality of rage and longing that begins anew from one to the next. I've stumbled upon self-reflection to the point of epiphany. Lucidity hurts. This is a curse. A dip into the spring of the gods, where the waters aren't meant for my mortal fragility.

One afternoon of my childhood I was walking home from elementary school, down the green and endless hill toward where I lived, and a squirm on the pavement provoked my glance. The bird was so fresh its eyes were closed. Its skin suctioned to the precious bones that jerked as it writhed, and its beak remained ajar in some kind of unquenchable pain or attempt to scream. I knew it wouldn't be retrieved by a parent after its fall from grace. Odd, I thought, that no tall trees lie in proximity. Perhaps an abandoned snack, or a runt. But it was sunny outside, and I'd loved animals as much as any little girl. The baby remained in the palm of my hand, sheltered past the park and through the driveway, careful as I opened the door.

We made her a home in a breathable plastic atrium with bedding and recently-shed rabbit fur. Snails and caterpillars had lived here before. I can't remember what the bird was fed, but it was given to her (?) through a dropper, and she'd lap it up. I didn't think she'd survive, but there was no way I'd have abandoned her there. I imagined the baby being squashed under the car of a tire, her pitiful bones stuck between the grooves of rubber until a bump in the road or a heavy rain shook them away. They'd spread across miles of road; more than the bird had probably travelled in life.

She'd been on her way out from the start. So lacking in fortune, so sad. Nothing could have been done, but when she finally died it brought rue, not relief. My caretaking was just an alternate means of death that extended what might have been a quick blade plucked from the meadow. Why did I bother? My grandfather once said that they'd given him increasingly profound views of the lake on increasingly high floors at the care facility, as he'd grown ill. To say that funerals are for the living is a cliché, but who cares about a painless death? I used lament over any type of ending; every facet of myself was open and turning in perpetuity. But a good writer knows when to stop tinkering; a good painter puts the brush down when it feels right. I wish I'd known that the most unexpected part of getting older was confronting last times, finalities, the end of things.

A river of intoxication down her pharynx, a dream in the mouthpiece of the pipe, fractured antilife until the devil gets wind of it. I'm not with her anymore but I think about her often; in fact, her face is hung on the wall above my kitchen table where I see her every morning. I want to reach into the canvas and put my mouth to her ear: "Die." ✦

＋　　＋　　＋　　＋　　＋　　＋　　＋　　＋　　＋

ENDINGS ARE SOMETHING CHRISTIANITY IS AFRAID
of, in the way that other systems of belief receive death
with more elegance and complex interpretation. In the
afterlife you are promised eternal suffering or eternal elation. I can't get with the program. I am an atheist, then,
not because I am interested in denial, but because the
promise of anything forever is just untrue.

I went to Vacation Bible School and attended Sunday
school until I was ten. I'd been given the option to opt-
out, and I took it (my mother and stepfather were never
dogmatic, and I could have left earlier had it occurred to
me). Agnosticism wasn't strong enough to describe my
early distaste of god and worship. The more I tried to
engage, the more concerned I felt about being told to put
trust in an abstract entity. I never really believed in a god
but alternatives weren't presented to me. I tried again in
middle school, when the popular girls all went to Christian sleepaway camp. I was so eager to be loved by them
so I tagged along, eager in general but feeling mostly isolated throughout. A "church leader" there (one of the girl's
mothers, in fact) asked us to write letters to god and read
them herself later that night. It was an artless endeavor;

her method lacked basic critical thinking. The believers I encountered and saw in the immediate world around me had no grace; the ones I encountered in art and literature glowed with elation and rapture, populating ancient stories and suspending my developing sensibility in emotional journeys that, eventually, I'd find, were too pure to have occurred in any version of reality I'd ever known.

The demand for compliance and the ensuing, inevitable surveillance encountered an adolescent mind, charged with imagining different ways of living and thinking. A world without reason unfurled before me.

The way writers make sense (or nonsense) of their memories is to dive into them. I'd always been told to write a story to be a writer; now I tell others to use artistry of language to work their way out of a problem.

My early internet experience comprised hours of research reading theories that claimed to disprove the Christian bible—it was quite too early for me to recognize that the chorus of "hard facts" and "research" was coming from the singular voice of a homogenous community of incels-in-progress who would, a decade later, return as an angry male opposition on my various social channels. But at the time they furiously typed and I listened because I wanted to explain away my disbelief. Anything outside the syllabus of my duties (school) was a curiosity because it was discovered by me rather than fed to me. It was a time when a girl still imagined what it would be like to orchestrate the contents of a day, when the idea of autonomy presented the glow of possibility. So much both above and below the green, green Earth began to stir.

I've also never believed in horoscopes, mostly just that the climate and season of one's birth has obvious effects on the kind of person they will come to be. But I've always bore my Scorpio classification lovingly, and I remember when I was younger, I admired all of the birthstone-related knickknacks when I'd accompany my mother to Hallmark near our house. Mood rings, incense, other cultural realms appropriated to nod to a post-religious type of 1990s American spirituality.

My birth stone is topaz according to some sources (the ones I encountered in childhood), and I wore a tiny "topaz"-colored gold piece of glass on my hand like a proclamation. So all kinds of belief exist and operate in this world; we've made them up as we've gone along. ✦

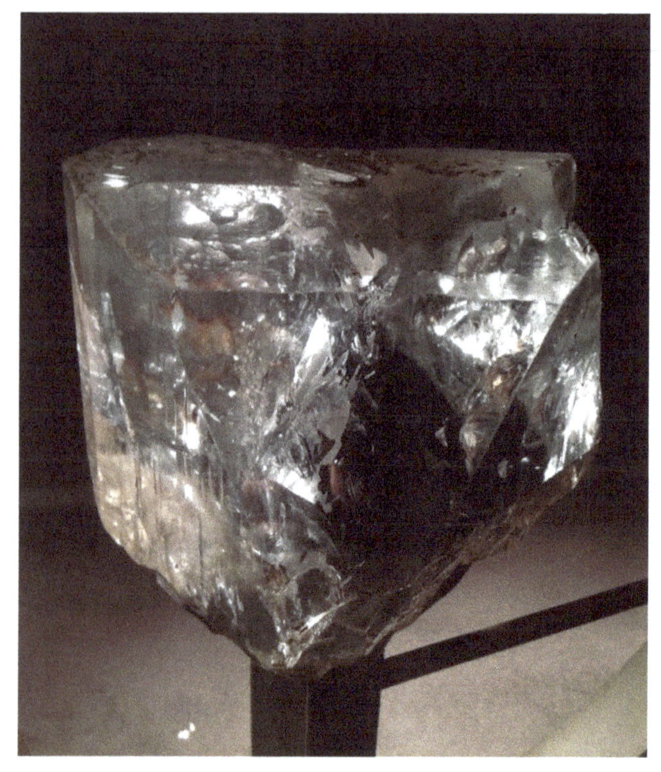

Topaz Crystal from Minas Gerais or Santa Maria de Itabira, Brazil. n.d. 9.4 x 7.5 x 9 in. (24x19x23 cm). The American Museum of Natural History, New York

CHAPTER 6

MY TARNISHED LEATHER COWBOY BOOTS SILENT against the carpet in the larkshadow-lined hall of stones and gems. I felt gauche and new to Earth while gazing upon roomfuls of knowledge and bits of our world so ancient and unwilling to sway in even the harshest storm. The American Museum of Natural History has rooms devoid of guests atop its cityblock green, especially on a weekday morning, and it's raining. Anyone whose been here is familiar with the old dioramas and the midcentury installations (though with many updated wall texts and labels). Some of the agedness of the place amuses me: the maroon shades of the carpet and the wood paneling. Tiny sculpture of a person on plastic farmland waiting to be set up straight. Dead flies and dust particles trapped behind the glass. And in a more updated portion of the museum…a taxidermized capybara!!! The place is massive, and I imagine its upkeep is something to behold. Other aspects of the museum I meet with a critical eye. But it's the earth and space sciences part that I love.

Before the Hall of Gems and Minerals underwent a massive renovation, reopening in June 2021, it was dark and, I felt, appropriately cavelike with deep indigo carpeting. Gems were spotlit and communicated space-bending magic. I gravitated toward a part of the room that glowed. A person like any other who loves shiny things. The stone on the pedestal was uncased, solitary as it harvested any glance of light from its surroundings, like an angel. It was so bright it seemed to ring.

(I understand anything worth regarding to be worthy of overthinking: the disturbed curl of tornado around its eye or dust in the garden. We spend so much time trying to decipher what should and shouldn't produce ekphrasis [on the Web: "It's really not that deep, bro"], when really we'd be better off banishing the distinction and thinking too much into everything. With all our agency, all the capacity we have…to interpret and see the world in the designs of our thoughts. This stone is not the product of human creation but from a point of aesthetic theory/environmentalism/history/provenance/wanting to observe, why ignore something so special?).

Below the surface of green Earth, topaz forms in metamorphic zones and at the end of a metamorphosis, when magma cools and shapeshifts into igneous rock. The timespans of these processes extend past human life, taking hundreds or thousands of years. Slow and circumstantial, hidden away. As is the case with all precious gems, topaz has signified different things to the people of our world across time, but has most consistently registered as a status and commodity of wealth. In the 1730s, a couple hundred years after Portugal colonized the land composing Brazil, the land was plundered for its topaz deposits. Time crunches between the characters in these sentences and expands in the spaces between words.

The topaz it sang a wordless dirge as I circled it in the room. I wanted to see how its interpretation of the world extended through so many jagged angles, hundreds of them, even thousands all at once. I felt incapable aside the unflinching glamor. I ignited the gas of feeling onto it, emoting. Photograph after photograph I took of this stone, trying to document it thoroughly so as never to forget how it reallocated light like phantom glow under the water of a cave. The phone, as it is today, captures so little, though I find that the photographs I take help me to maintain my memories and create a narrative to my life for the moments when I feel lost. I scroll through them under the covers. I look at them on the airplane. I lament the phones I lost whose photos weren't saved on the Cloud or a backup device. Patchworks of life that will remain barren in the great photostream of my life.

Just years before this encounter at the AMNH, I'd dreamt of reflective and prismatic jellyfish as lovely as topaz in the sky on a cloudy day, had attempted to take photos of them, unsuccessfully, repetitiously. The redemptive quality of this encounter, that I was able to document now what I'd been unable to back then, was not lost on me. At times we are given the chance to repent and should take it.

I imagined looking out from within this stone—from its unchanging solitude—its surfaces in hazy and distorted images would remind of the view behind eyes perpetually on the brink of weeping. In fact, topaz is not particularly refractory, absorbing light, vessel-like. It seemed unfair that I was unable to reach into it, could only (if it weren't a cardinal sin) extract feeling from its surface. A topaz crystal from Minas Gerais, Brazil, or possibly from Santa Maria de Itabira, curator Dr. George E. Harlow of the Museum tells me over email: "The ambiguity is because it was found on display without attribution in 1971 as the previous mineral hall was being disassembled." The curation of such a museum and the acquisition of an object like a topaz is unknown to me. I imagine it is fueled by a similar passion to the one that strikes the heart of conservators who must command knowledge of so many areas, foremost being chemistry and art. These people are holy to me, holding together threads of our world that, when combined, launch the education of the public and our understanding of art toward undiscovered realms.

Any eye might be drawn toward something so bright and miraculous. The arrangement of molecules that brought this specimen into its final form had no dependency on our interference, but was brought to the surface by our hands so that we may see what lies beyond our sight. I tend to bend in awe of the presence of something so old, whose stories and visions cannot genuinely be known by me but only contrived by me. Though, had it remained intact below the stone from which it was mined, light would not have had the opportunity to pass through. Its concealed potential would remain potent, knifelike. I sometimes think that which haunts our world—both beyond and within—loses duende once exposed. It burns out and crumbles under the weight of dissection. What

I'm trying to suggest is that this spillage of the specters wandering my mind might deflate my experience of them. Then they will die and rot within me. But any piece of writing is hope. ✦

✦   ✦   ✦   ✦   ✦   ✦   ✦   ✦   ✦

WHEN I WAS IN SCHOOL, I FOUND SOLACE IN PRIVATE conversations with my English teachers. I'd sit in their classrooms (or the library) during lunch; seek answers... Their sensitivity to characters in literature and vast interpretation of images and feelings made them open to the problems faced by young folks. One middle school teacher was sympathetic to my anxiety around anonymous MySpace bullying. A college professor helped me through the drug addiction and eventual death of a friend.

Near the end of high school, my teacher taught an entire unit on existentialism. He had us read a few of the greatest hits to illustrate the foundations of the existentialist school of thought: *Waiting for Godot*, *The Stranger*, more stories than theory, which I found incredibly effective since I had not yet had the opportunity to rigorously explore the latter. We looked at stage adaptations of Beckett's play and discussed how different iterations of the play's set gave a visual language to the absurd. So, then, the antidote to meaninglessness was art. I could be the agent of my own meaning; the answers would come from my perception and understanding of the world and those around me. No systems of belief or patterns of faith would need to open my path into each new

year of my life. It was the most sacred thing I'd ever learned.
Near the beginning of Estragon and Vladimir's banter:

ESTRAGON

The Bible . . . (He reflects.) I must have taken a look at it.

VLADIMIR

Do you remember the Gospels?

ESTRAGON

I remember the maps of the Holy Land. Coloured they were. Very pretty. The Dead Sea was pale blue. The very look of it made me thirsty. That's where we'll go, I used to say, that's where we'll go for our honeymoon. We'll swim. We'll be happy.

VLADIMIR

You should have been a poet.

ESTRAGON

I was. (Gesture towards his rags.) Isn't that obvious?
Silence.

VLADIMIR

Where was I . . . How's your foot?

Perhaps my own tendency to sentimentalize everything sheds a tender light on this moment within an otherwise abysmal play. It seems so sophomoric to mention a piece of literature which is, I imagine, standard to the American High School Experience. But I love Estragon's unintentional sidestep into waxing lyricism. The interpretation of a map as a work of art (it surely is, see chapter in here on Alexander Si). The momentary gleam of a hopeful imagination and ensuing self-deprecation. An artist's mark, coming into the dialogue of the play like the hand of god. ✦

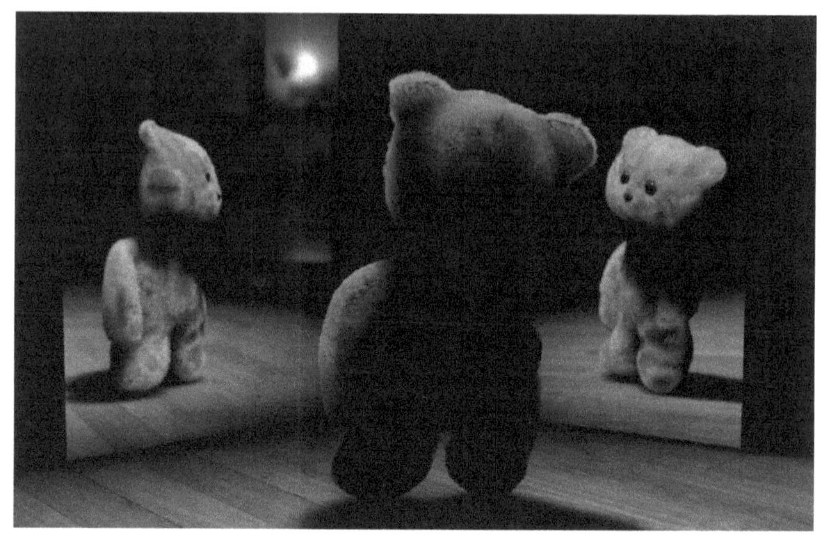

Juan Antonio Olivares (b. 1988, Puerto Rico). *Moléculas*, 2017. High-definition video, color, sound, 10 min. Whitney Museum of American Art; purchase with funds from the Film, Video, and New Media Committee. Image courtesy the artist

CHAPTER 7

My eagerness for domestic bliss had crumbled so quickly...like walking through the gaping mouth of a cave and into someone else's lair. I needed to emerge into undiscovered realms anew. Shifting lavender to twilight blue; eruption of infinite. The caustic shock of being in a "situation" and becoming the girl who now others might be pitying. The basic premise was of a young and failed romance, so typical that even the most floral language could not render it unique. Falling into a received narrative; how gauche. Cue sadness theme. How the tethers of young twentihood restrain us whether we'd like them to or not. I'd began to dread going home and realized I'd make any excuse to stay at a friend's house. Too late for the subway; too tired for the subway; subway schedule is too fucked up. When I'd began making plans to start anew alone, I felt like I was going away to the country, seeking a perpetual aloneness and redefinition of my own creative practice. To rename the things I'd always loved outside the narrow parameters of he who was dying so desperately to be like me. One night I schlepped to The BogArt galleries. My dear friend Chuks Ndulue cast his prose across the room. Art is always co-directing my life. *That's* why I'd come here. I felt it. Life was dynamic for others, I noticed. The quotidian as practice; the fluid shapelessness of life on your own terms. People leaned against one another and closed their eyes to perceive the seduction of poetics. They got up to go to the bathroom; made sure the factory doors clanked just slightly on the way out. They removed and rehung a painting from the wall. I helped myself to generous pours of white wine and passed through gallery after gallery. A handsome person in overalls smiled at me. The carnelian bloom of a tiny oceanic shore at high tide glowing for only a moment under the passage of the lighthouse's touch. When I emerged from the studios, the sky over these streets was wide and windy. I walked to find dinner and sang an old Bruce Cockburn song as I tiptoed across a bike rack like a balance beam. Happiness at being away, so far removed from all *that*.

Growing. I needed to find a way to communicate, to tell him that I was leaving him, a thought that paralyzed me almost enough to halt me from doing it completely. Whenever I'd leave the apartment, I was fidgety, looking at my cell phone and mindlessly opening one application after another. Exiting out of them. A few weeks ago, I'd hidden in the bathtub and curled onto the floor with my knees against my chest. No text messages, why do I keep taking my phone out of my pocket… Check my phone again a few seconds later. Sometimes in that bathroom, in December, I'd open the window at the end of the tub to allow the tiles to grow cold. If you sink through tile you reach somewhere larger with more time: Victorian Seaside. Hokkaido onsen. Elsewheremaxxing. The comradery of light emitted by windows across the courtyard suggested only that I'd shut myself out from happiness in this world. The light from other windows shot up and down the narrow rectangle. A few times I laid in the tub with my favorite stuffed animal and fell asleep. I frantically clutched a dull kitchen knife to my chest and closed the shower curtain. There were water spills all over the Persian rug. I had no idea what was going on. Tens of thousands of unread emails. At the courtyard's floor our superintendent was moving trash. One time he'd yelled at me to get off the roof. We were only beginning the finale of a death spiral in America. A scab stuck to my corduroys when I took them off after work in the evening and the wound began anew.

I escaped to museums when it was time to learn to leave for good. The Whitney was exhibiting a Grant Wood retrospective. I didn't spend as much time there as I'd planned, wasn't as affected in the presence of *American Gothic* which was no huge surprise I guess. There was time enough that day to see the rest of the museum, and the halls sang so brightly next to the Hudson River. A film was playing in the theater. Had to put my phone away in there. Immediately, I transitioned into the lifelong habit of picking my cuticles, but then I settled in and disappeared.

Moléculas is a film by Juan Antonio Olivares that is backdropped, or perhaps foregrounded, by a monologue. The tone of the speaker is sage; its hills are curved by the gentle brush of a hand. He talks of his mother, his first memory of her, of seeing a pile of snow, of how living near the copper mines aged her beyond her years and of how he always knew his mother loved him more than she loved his brother. This display of preference had been painful, canyonlike.

The voice in *Moléculas* is carried by the most devastatingly expressive teddy bear there ever was. He appears on the psychotherapist's couch, missing an arm, speaking freely. He walks before the mirror and reviews his reflection. Through the window of a room with a desk, a field of glaciers. He remembers when he learned of his mother's death, standing in the phone booth and speaking with his brother. He had just moved away from home. She's just died. He feels "a rush of pain." A bathtub fills with water and overflows, drowning the room with sorrow. The bear's arm drops to the sidewalk with several pieces of bodily fluff. Memories appear now behind a window dripping with condensation, obscuring what transpires before but represented by the film's most vivid colors: a view of the Earth from space, dance of molecules. He tries to understand how the living can relate to death: "It's here that you have to do things so that when you're gone you don't leave behind those deep..." trailing off. The bear's tail twitches as he dreams on his stomach. There are calculated motions over the operating table. The bear swings upside down, clipped to a laundry line before a sky of stars. He sees himself reflected infinitely in the mirror and explodes.

Even with this lean description of the film's moments, I think you'll intercept the evolution of thought that Olivares presents. What I say is speculation, but my connection to the work is unbreakable. There is one transformation after another, as water becomes ice becomes gas, is shuddered into the universe. In the event of great pain, part of ourselves—physical and otherwise—becomes separated from us, scattered beyond us, transformed. The narrator...

he was transformed by death; by the unchangeable, foundational family dynamic that shaped his own life and that of his brother; by the wrenching inner-tension bloomed of having moved away from home. By the inability to disentangle oneself from the torments and evils of globalized capitalism; the destruction of the nature which raised us before our eyes; its effects on how we love and live. It's so hot now. So what is born of despair?

"When death changes us, we enter another type of life."

Here is the possibility of creating meaning without depending on the way things are in order to make sense of them. *Moléculas* brims with regret, but suggests the potential of regret to outlive its vessel. Nothing leaves the world for good. This cannot be forgotten. Think of replicating the fabric of life, of recycling and renewing. I'd always interpreted the phantom limbs of my neglected paths to represent failure. Before a brush with death, I felt the end of my life approaching me, the opportunities I'd left untapped—to be a better friend and lover and daughter, to leave the bar an hour earlier, to break the self-destructive patterns of thought that diminished my will to create—sequestered my life into a small chalice of achievements. My wrongs pained me into submission.

All the possibilities of other me's banished. I peered into this chalice and swirled the liquid. I made habit of writing down the problem as such: "Jan. 21: Growing anxious at the thought of going unpublished for any particular amount of time, as if I'll disappear. Want to be constantly announcing to myself that I am here. Not sure if my life means anything otherwise."

I imagine myself pouring the contents of the chalice out, watching the ephemeral Naomi slowly spread thin and sink into the ground. Perhaps it was the case that she could have been reconstituted as seed and scattered across soil. *Moléculas* into something new.

The practice of filmmaking is especially admirable to me because so many creative elements must be weighed against one another at once: visual and auditory and the cinematic devices that fall within what writers might call the subtext. Olivares' subtle creative hand presents larger universal notions of death while honoring the particularities of the autobiographical storyline acting as foundation for the narrative. Setting these familial recordings against a dark, sweet, lonely animation generates a continuous negotiation of reality. We enter that magic place, a psychological in-between where viewer senses high stakes of "relatable" human experience while being whisked into an otherworld. It's hard to describe despite the vocalizing of such phenomena being the critic's job. Though I am no critic; I am just writing about my feelings at the end of the day.

Leaving the Whitney's small theater, I mashed the palms of my jacket to my eyes and pressed deeply into my skull. The fruition of another's impulse to create rippled the stagnancy of my life. Feeling the transformation as it occurs. It was an extraordinarily sun-filled corridor, and I, messianic in the wake of the encounter. Though it took a while for the colors to present themselves, the coming weeks grew vibrant. What I wanted to say was within my reach, or else I'd reach for it, but it was there. I appeared in the archway of my kitchen. After all… I mean to say that I am leaving. ✦

✦   ✦   ✦   ✦   ✦   ✦   ✦   ✦   ✦

ANY SERIOUS REORIENTATION TO THE WORLD SEARS off the outer layer of one's alien skin, for some time leaving behind a pulsing and slimy outer shell that will adapt to whatever's around and harden once again with time. I've never been one to shed naturally. A change in scenery, a new job, a new perspective: it always blows me out of the water, as I'm sure it does with so many of you. Bit of revival; semblance of an earlier form; unattainability of… a path going straight toward the dewy heavens. The idea of transformation as painful is a cliché, because the conditions of human life are never established and are only continuously jolted into action. I want to fall through these changes, to let my body be lacerated by whatever parts of my existence are significant enough to be collected and stored in my mind. I am beginning to feel the density of the air. I will be moved by the art I see and the experiences art gives; the chorus to my rebirth is supported by oils, negatives, megabytes, and millions of moments of human connection. Cut it down to affirmation if you need. I just want to know whether anything I had thought or felt or accomplished in my life had mattered. ✦

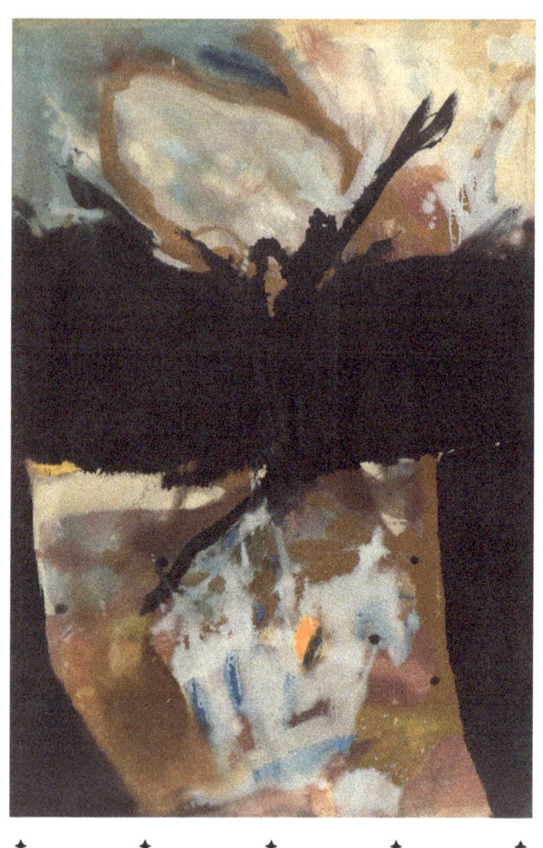

Helen Frankenthaler. *Trojan Gates*. 1955. Oil
and enamel on canvas. 6 ft. x 48 7/8 in. (182.9
x 124.1 cm). The Museum of Modern Art, New
York. Gift of Mr. and Mrs. Allan D. Emil

CHAPTER 8

An eruption bled into the world. A mass of black, *Trojan Gates*, pushes obliteration into a mess of color that tells me no story. I must figure one out. Post-transformation, now. Clutching through airwaves to see if fragment of paint of canvas have accidentally slipped into the wrong dimension. Frankenthaler's work is usually softer-edged, seeping toward the parameters of the frame like watercolor, more tempered into the canvas with turpentine. It stains, washes, waves in gardeny, earth-and-above hues that blend and whisper to one another and to you, if you stop to listen.

You should know that we bring our baggage to any interpretation of a work of art; any interpretation that matters, anyway. You recall your exaltations and sufferings, once-shapeless memories are kicked from the silt and their details strike like lightning before your eyes. Perhaps you cringe before an abstraction of rosy reds and soft whites because as a child, you once ate a bag of peppermint saltwater taffy and vomited at a Californian Wax Museum. Perhaps transient rainbows have peppered your dreams and reconjured in the silvery spectrum of a video artist's light pool. There is a place for attempts at objectivity, but not here. Not in the rebuilding of the self. I didn't begin to study art from an academic angle. I don't like it there; I deny them what they want. I want the facts to be right but the feelings to be mine.

This painting is an explosion into gestures of color whose stories cannot be described in generalizations but only in other works of art personal to the writer: Laurie smoking a joint in the convertible during a refracted sundown under the eerie breeze of a '70s suburb stalked by Michael Myers; Princess Kaguya of the Moon, escaping the shackles of noblewomanhood by planting things in the garden; small explosions of beauty that are only the beginning of a body in action.

You feel the artist's body move without inhibition, giving into impulse. It feels like the woman made a painting she wanted to make, like she wasn't attempting unity or perfection in that way that I feel Pollock—someone by whom she was greatly inspired and who I strongly dislike!—was in all his aggression and macho-postured "automatism."

When I began researching her, I found the timbre of her voice to be composed and its cadence to be quite commanding. I also discovered that I was drawn to her work made in the '50s and '60s, and snatched Alexander Nemerov's biography about her off the bookstore shelf almost right after it came out in 2022. She grew up in Manhattan, and as a fellow woman living in the City in her 20s (now entering my 30s!), I devoured the social aspects of the narrative as much as the rest of it.

Frankenthaler created her art in association with those who appear in histories of the 1950s and '60s New York art scene: Grace Hartigan, Tibor de Nagy, Barbara Rose, David Smith, Robert Motherwell, Hans Hoffman, Clement Greenberg. Nemerov's book confirms how indebted Helen felt to Pollock. Much to my dismay as a fan, she expressed her work as a direct descendant of his. Nemerov writes, "Helen transforms Pollock's heroic and self-destructive totems… [her] sensitivity allowed her to grant ordinary experience—faltering, incomplete, apparently meaningless—the primping vanity of beauty." There we go. She was friends with dear Frank O'Hara, too, and *his* friend James Schuyler (one of my favorite poets) said that a painting of Helen's "drift[ed] like winds." Frankenthaler was indeed in fine company.

The first time I saw her work must have been at the Seattle Art Museum, a stones' throw from where I was born. Later I spotted her around New York, as I got acquainted with the City's museum circuit. I saw *Trojan Gates* at MoMA's 2017 "Making Space: Women Artists and Postwar Abstraction" curated by Starr Figura, Sarah Hermanson Meister, and Hillary Reder. In witnessing it, I saw the moment of obliteration, in which the painting reveals itself, where her rarely-highlighted black pigment explodes into color. This is what holds the composition together. I like to read it as the destruction of the canon, Frankenthaler's arrival in the arena of genius, which was in her time, and even ours, so often reserved for men. In a similar vein, why is my brain so frustratingly stunted by what it's perceived over the course of my life that I have to remind myself that my emotive reckoning is not just the condition of my particular brand of womanhood or more precisely, of my experience as a projection onto not only Frankthaler's work but her *life*—but also a greater condition of humanity?

You'll see that I've captioned the work according to how MoMA lists the materials: "oil and enamel on canvas." This omits the aspect of the work that makes it magnificent. If you happen to be in New York City and you visit the Museum's galleries during a time when the painting is hung, go find it. Look closely and you'll see a matchstick stuck, partially covered in black paint. How patches of black seem to obscure other kinds of colorful movement and gesture but how the presence of tension is still visually gratifying if you like that kind of thing. And if we ascribe meaning of the title to the painting then I wonder which perspective is inhabited here; trickster or the tricked? Trickster. There is something (sheepishly) dangerous about how freely the work moves. Unguided. Towards fury. Explosion of color and end of war. The final say. And in thinking of fury and the memorialization of memory, place, history, I inevitably get to thinking about Helen and the overwhelming disdain I might have for these circles of artists and writers who easily fell into the self-feeding canon of which we are finally bored to death.

My love for Modernism and its aesthetic indicators and variations—as I do—is constantly compromised by my awareness of its global mission as a colonizing one. A macho one, a patriarchal one. One co-opted by the military-industrial complex (and I am not only talking about Cold War politics). One that wants to be an easy story so badly that it constantly tells on itself. So then how to review a painting without the soft lens of academia? I think de-canoning oneself is akin to relearning to move my limbs.

The mind's composition must remain limber. Within the its spongy labyrinth, deconstruction and reassociation begins at one ending and ends where something new has just occurred.

Everything seemed beyond me. I reach the edge of the ocean and stand on the cliff. Decide whether to jump. Violet of inside. I fall through a corridor of memory. Down and further out, I look toward now- unreachable horizons, upon some far-off happier seas, that only suggest all the world had been mine to sculpt, and I'd let it wither and scream oblivion. Between narrows and treacherous whirpools. My vessel's walls are impenetrably thick. I massage my temples. I hear the passive creaking of the boards but no lapping of waves. Out the back of the boat, the water stirs, and up above, the Cascade Mountains point without question toward the sky where the shades of kelp and glacier project. The heavens an antique map of my world. We were just guessing as we felt our way along the shore, divvying the world up into arbitrary pieces that—if not a bad idea at the time—would grow to be later, in ways unexpected. Gazing into the saintly realm of the sky and all its ranges. In fact, I can see everything: the sky is a mirror. I am within it and perhaps my gazing defines it.

The past always gathers together like a prayer. Shape the earnestness to continue finding life in the creation and experience of art. As in time passes and I stroll through it, as in consciousness. Developing the knowing around what is first seen and felt. Frankenthaler as a purveyor of infinite expansion like the galaxy; Frankenthaler as a soft meditation that has returned to me over the course of these years. +

✦   ✦   ✦   ✦   ✦   ✦   ✦   ✦   ✦

THE FRANKENTHALERIAN EXPANSION OF EMOTION REminds me of transcending the perils of "experimental" prose, meaning, prose that manipulates language, time, distorts or conceals meaning in subtext, etc. The distinction of it from other writing meant to describe how some work was deemed accessible to the public and other work was not, and it was made by the general publishing industry—I am both within and outside of it—with the sweeping and patronizing assumption that a wide audience cannot engage and intercept unusual forms that they did not, for example, grow up with or receive through mainstream airwaves. I'm thinking about the things I learned about writing over the course of my school years. Spinning in the recollection of iconic histories that have entered my own bloodstream. Art criticism in the 20th century was generally not meant to express that which stirs within the writer. It was Clement Greenberg-ed into discussions of whether the writer's own history should even configure into the conversation, etc. The men of the industry (both surrounding and creating the art) circle-jerked their way into the history they solidified and the one we've received. This is the one that I know most intimately and the one I hope to be released from in these words I string together. Sprinting away from the things that bind me feels so pathtic; even writing in the shadow of writing feels patronizing.

This work is an experiment insomuch as I am experimenting with degrees of perceiving myself and rewriting impulsive image with extended, planned thought. And caring about anything here all depends on you. ✦

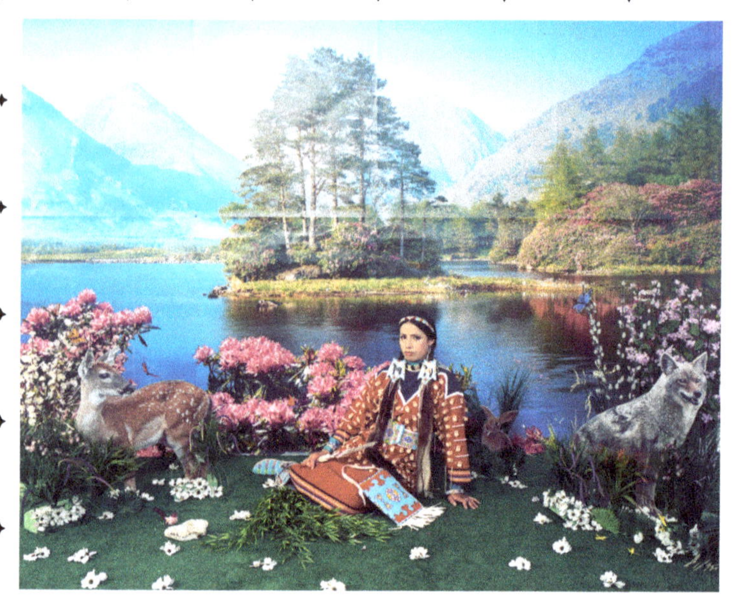

Wendy Red Star. *The Four Seasons (Spring)*. 2006. Archival pigment print on Museo silver rag mounted on Dibond. 35.5 x 37 in. each panel (90.17 x 94 cm). Nerman Museum of Contemporary Art, Johnson County Community College, Overland Park, Kansas (2014.06–2014.09)

CHAPTER 9

Wendy Red Star made a series of four photographs, one for each season. Donning traditional Crow regalia in each, she places herself in dioramas that darkly and bitingly replicate those at The American Museum of Natural History and its equivalents. Her shade of commentary is whiplike, acute, holds a mirror to the world.

The vibrancy of *The Four Seasons* is composed by both the garments Red Star showcases as well as the plastic technicolor palette of her mis-en-scene: astroturf, cardboard cutouts, backdrops creased from being factory folded and packaged. Intentional failures to produce a plausible reality, to stage a reproduction of a vignette that is, in its original form, a purposeful fumble to represent humanity or to represent the atrocities of a country that constantly gapes in the presence of its own moribund shadow. In an interview with *Aperture*, Red Star described that:

"Native people are represented as eradicated, like in Edward Curtis's *The Vanishing Race* (1904) project. It's worked pretty well. I think people are surprised when they find a Native person because in the consciousness of America it's like we don't exist. We are these mythical creatures."

If you've been to any natural history museum you've seen these dioramas before: they contain taxidermized animals in replicas of their natural habitats and scenes of global human culture using mannequins and (generally) plundered garments, tools, and other objects, as well as showcases of biological processes and the practices humans enact to try and harness the wild around them. I have as much criticism as I do awe for the museum in New York City (you see, it has just appeared in a previous chapter), which houses enough dioramas to view for hours upon hours, set in the dim lighting and hushed tones of an early museum morning during the off-season. I imagine most of us recognize the dioramas as public knowledge at their mention, and this calls on the unchecked authority of institutions that document the country's past, freezing the dimensionality and continued traditions of communities all over the land. AMNH includes placards that display corrective history and restorative justice, but yet, but yet…

In attempting to approach understanding of another person's experience of life, I seek information, a way to be less ignorant to the life of people. Accounts of injustice and of thievery and abuse must make you livid. Other people's pain… must enrage you and radicalize you. Make you see beyond the shiny language of theory and politic and into the hearts of others. A potent artwork with the power to transform its viewers must be honored: I'm thinking about it. Shout it from across the ocean between you and me, so it is understood and then echoes beyond.

Centered in Red Star's *Seasons*, the subject, the artist herself, regarding me as readily as I regard her. Her gaze into the camera's lens, and, by extension, me, is undivided and shall remain so in perpetuity, because the work exists on. The frame of a photograph extends across time. The artist penetrates the fourth-wall, a declaration. And springtime…this part of the series is my favorite. The seasons are an infinite wellspring of meaning and imagery.
There are endless staple notions about spring, of rebirth and renewal to accompany it. I imagine what comes to life around me, in the field or between cracks in the pavement: life reckons with heavy dew and arises, coming. Perhaps I'll be so overwhelmed by the arousal of senses that I'll forget what hasn't returned. If summer intoxicates us

with the ripeness and sunshine, then spring lulls us into a goofy sense of wellbeing, perhaps simply because we are no longer cold. Some color on the ground. Red Star's deer and wolf and rabbit appearing in close harmony, the giant, symphonic Disneyfication of the coming of spring. Because, what if I failed to be there, to record what was happening and later, did not know what was lost along the way?

Red Star also appears in her older works, in which she identifies a depiction of the self and recasts it. Her work reimagines colonialist and post-colonialist stories of westward expansion in the United States. Her White Squaw series, for example, is based off of the series of trashy and artistically void books of the same name. Red Star satirizes the original book covers by inhabiting the objectified, sexualized caricature of the half-Oglala, half-European protagonist and extending its absurdity. In one work, she licks the edge of a tomahawk. In another, she picks her nose with an arrow.

Her newer investigations have a slightly different approach: she handwrites informative notations on historical photographs of Crow chiefs or collaborates with her young daughter in photographs of vibrant Crow clothing.

Her artistic practice moves between both the correction of historical lies and the self-documentation that assures the same mistakes will not become a pattern and poison the future. I am struck by this kind of decisive action in art. It reveals how one's practice breathes.

Her collection of diorama photographs (and the series of book covers) are the kinds of art that stir a familiar and uncomfortable feeling in my chest. Degrees of guilt and shame. Ideas and histories bigger than can be perceived. A rage that asks to be turned into action. Because the art that I like presents a question in the form of an answer.

In her photograph, the subject is asking the viewer what they see. Surrounded by the unperishable textures and plastics that come as product of systems of production which are entirely out of control and overproducing. There is just always more and more. The photograph is a pause, in more ways than one. The re-presentation of the familiar and outrageous into something we might recognize and, in recognizing, come to want to change. +

✦   ✦   ✦   ✦   ✦   ✦   ✦   ✦   ✦

"IT IS INDEED SOME KIND OF ENDLESS SHORE UPON which I stand and try to breathe and discover, what will matter to me in the long run, at the end of my days, when I am… Every day I wait to feel that I have arrived. I've glimpsed it in flashes, in moments that I don't realize are the highlights of my life… Every day is a chance to rise above the rule of the words, the words in my head, to make them mine."

The artists in this book gleam in the damp light of my blood moon; these chapters are my songs for them. For I am born in mid-November, after all. To participate in the stream of discourse that surrounds them or to begin building one. Yearning to see these pages flutter into the long stream of other people's words and become entwined with it all. I like to think of the history of art as a series of responses; each artist is just paying homage to all that has come before. It's my truth. My problem is I am so terrible at writing about people, but so fascinated by what they create. When I begin to describe someone I admire, it becomes a sopping love letter of praise, lacking dimension (or if I reject them; a curse lacking the nuance to be affective). When I consider their art, possibilities abound, I feel that perhaps it is a window for me to understand who someone is in my favorite way. An artist of any kind who does not see themself or their ideas or impulses reflected in the work they create is suspicious to me. That doesn't mean that the things we make are extensions of ourselves, but that they manifest what evolves inside. ✦

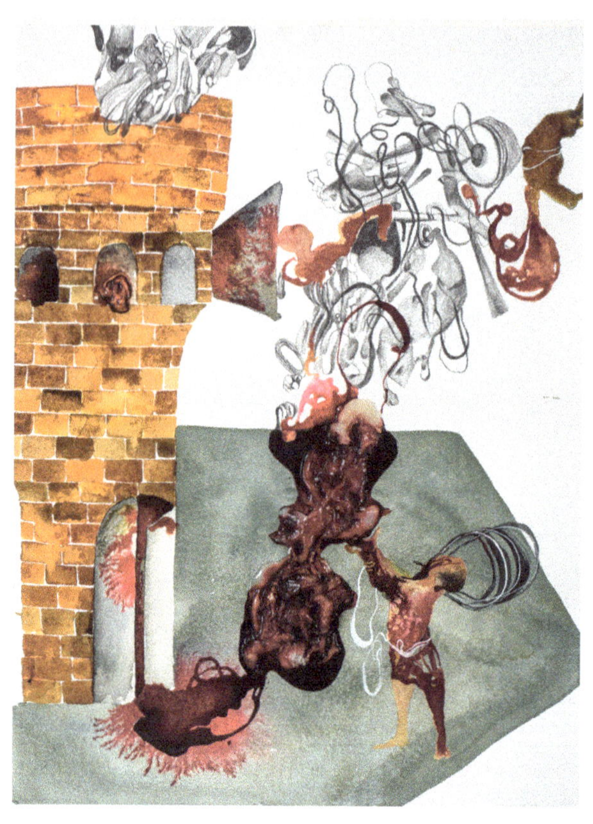

Shiva Ahmadi. *Castle*. 2018. Mixed media on paper, 20 x 15 in. (50.8 x 38.1 cm). Courtesy of the artist

CHAPTER 10

THERE ARE TIMES IN MY LIFE WHEN I'VE PENT UP MY rage until it crippled me. I've seen so many women experience a similar phenomenon, where they'd explode into fantasies of murder and freedom and ecstasy, dream of a place far away.

I shake off this rage, I eat it, and regurgitate it. Plant it into the ground. I want to drag men's faces along the pavement and into a bloody pulp, until all that remains is one last tooth hanging by a sinewy piece of gum. If you hold the strand up to against the sky, it catches the light, still dripping in saliva. Pick it up. Its color shifts from white to blushy rose to carnelian, depending on its position. The tooth spins and spins one way and now the other, like a weathervane.

Do you plan to tell me something, or what?

So indecisive, so inconsequential, this tooth, this stretched out piece of patriarchal tissue from which the little bone dangles. Hate to see how long a tooth becomes when unhoused. I regard it closely when a question arises: from whence does madness spring? From an inability to escape or make them see what it is you see and how you experience the world?

Don't talk to me at all. For awhile, I stopped dressing for summer because to you, it was only an invitation. In the high noon of a heatwave, eyes ablaze. I'd like to undress *you* and grill you on Cadillac chrome. Dreaming of basking alone on this street, under the sun, no threat, no problem. Blowing bubbles. Running through the streams of water erupting from the gushing fire hydrants. They make the pavement so wet. The ground glistens. The hot anger that I conceal slowly dissolves from the surface of my skin, I am shedding myself from the inside out. I turn my face to the sun.

Sometimes an artwork just gives me a feeling. Dip into and out of it. Take it and run to see what images I might conjure. In the case of Shiva Ahmadi's paintings, there's this ecstatic blossom of intellect, politics, anger, and fever. The rage transitions into a display of wide, open creation. It makes me feel an unhindered, pure wave of creativity and celebreality. An unquenchable yearning for excellence and for the kind of knowledge that makes you feel powerful.

The first time I saw Ahmadi's work was with Mina at the 2016 exhibition "Global/Local 1960–2015: Six Artists From Iran" at New York University's Grey Gallery. Ahmadi deals primarily in painting, sculpture, and animation. The images in her work are influenced by Persian, Indian, and Middle Eastern styles and patterns, and their details and contexts are particular to our current political climates. It is hard to perceive what takes place in her work upon first glance; it reveals itself slowly. In her paintings, I notice the narrative nature of the work as it floats suspended in backdrops washed in the palette of the surface of the earth. Her compositions tell stories of factories, figures tossing bombs, carnage, rivers and pools, tools of enslavement and servitude, of the masses and those who want to rule them, Ahmadi's two primary series of sculptures include oil barrels and pressure cooker bombs, all ornately hand-etched or painted and tampered with through modifications that both elevate—elegant metallic detailing—and politicize—explosive gauges in the metal or bloodlike streams pouring from orifices of the sculpture. She achieves this balance between supreme aesthetic beauty and sharp critical commentary that leaves me, time and time again, absolutely thunderstruck.

When I spoke to Ahmadi years ago, we generated material for an interview for *BOMB Magazine*. I was unsurprised by her way of telling stories that became a unique form of narrative artistry in her relaying of them.

"My life was hugely affected by the uncertainty and instability brought by the Iranian Revolution of 1979 and the subsequent eight-year, Iran-Iraq war. During the war we experienced city bombings for a period of time. As a child I was terrified of the sound of an explosion and the unknowns that came with it. One day my mom told me that if I hid underneath the big, sturdy, German-made table in the kitchen, I would be fine even if a bomb dropped on our house! I believed her! After that, anytime I heard helicopters, I would grab a book and hide under the table. Books and stories took me to another world and made me forget the ugliness of our situation. One of the books I read during this time was the Farsi version of George Orwell's *Animal Farm*."

Decades later, Ahmadi lives and works in California's Bay Area. Her multiperspectived understanding of the world is at once malleable by her and omniscient. I feel as if I can listen closely enough and hear fifty words bloom from each one she expresses, in the same way that her artwork bursts of opposing and multifaceted texture, material, shape, and depth. I asked her to tell me five words to describe how she feels upon viewing her own work, and she said: "Whimsy, red, playland, anxiety, throw up.

This chorus of meaning arising from her singular voice is a phenomenon I experience only in hearing the cantations of women, their washes of lyricism and blades of acute observation. I love women (and those aren't men) so deeply and with fervor. I believe that we see panoramically and through the pinhole of the microscope at once. We have to. We were taught through our playgrounds and books and shows of our prescribed and somehow inherent need to caretake, to nurture, to love animals and dolls and inanimate wonders brought to life with courageous imagination, before we were shown the possibility of creative genius. We came prepared. They tell us we "carry life," the vessels of mortality, continuing, knowing that the fruition of a dream is often rooted in pain. That carrying life defines womanhood no more than sex determines gender. But anything to keep people at bay, bioessentialism says anything to ensure that nothing ever changes.

The anger rising from my womanhood is multifarious. It contains the universe, harnessing the cycles of the world in which we move but which only women can control. My body is connected to the sea and the sky: I am pulled and pull the forces that chain me to the earth. I remember what it was like to be bound to something, to someone. To the ideas of society built by and for men. And a man is just a product of it, you helpless cog. All the times that you patronized me can be written off as a hilarious underestimation of my power. Do you remember when you told me my work did nothing to prove that I was equipped to write about art? The you is *you*, but it's also the umbrella. You see, I have grown my nails and sharpen them on the edge of a switchblade. While you sleep, I will squat lightly over your flaccid, soft body, sliding my fingers down through the filthy and meaningless layers of your flesh and muscle, pulling apart ligaments to locate organs, which I will consume in order to dominate you and diminish you into the excrement that leaves my body and returns to the earth. Tack you down to the bedframe so you can't squirm. I do it better than you. I demolish more than you can dream of, more of the world than you knew existed. The theorists will call it a feminist revenge thriller, but it's really just my fantasy. Can't you tell?

You wouldn't be able conjure names for the things I'm about to do to you. The body that seemed so capable—if not helpless—in its reactions to me, in life, falls apart in my hands, now. You thought that my presentation was for your benefit? Nothing you could do to me could disintegrate me; your need to contain my extraordinary heights only increases me. Anger rising, pouring forth into the world more fully than the machinations of war.

Understand that a woman's anger, and especially that of nonbinary angels and other fluid and forming genders and genderless people who walk the earth propelled by the strength of their identities—unlike war created by, waged by, and directed by men in power—does not level the territory. When we are angry, our wide spectrum of emotion is cast into the world. Our highest elation and our darkest suffering. Something new emerges. This is why I write. We're not stuck in the valley of the damned. That's what you created, how you saw hell, with all your limitations. Lack of imagination is what I see when I peer down to the world created by the most terrible ones.

The rest of us, we're somewhere higher now. Ahmadi's work lays claim to that. I am not suggesting anything of the artists intention; only showing what it makes me feel.

In her *Castle* from 2018: Is what I see the detritus of human gore? Yes. The wasteland laid by global conflict. And still, something speaks to me personally, the chunky, carnelian multimedia layered upon the canvas itching a sensory scratch, performing for me some elated expression of release? Yes—pain works its way into such narrow cracks: three chords passing in a song, déjà vu, the place I stood in the bathroom when I cried for your attention, yellow so regal I mistook it for gold. Inside a woman, one thousand choirs sing a language unheard. When we speak, you should listen. Perhaps what we have to say will change you for the better. Ahmadi's characters tell you they have something to say: faceless tyrants and worshippers bound to themselves and intricately to others, pure carnage, phantomlike vignettes unconnected to the ground of our Earth but still, painfully, belonging to us. ✦

✦   ✦   ✦   ✦   ✦   ✦   ✦   ✦   ✦

I'M STANDING IN FRONT OF THE MIRROR AND THROUGH the bathroom window the sun sets aside the church's steeple. The top half of it was lobbed off some time ago. The room is a simple box; imagine how exposed I would be standing here if the building's protective wall crumbled away. I need a cup of water. There is a glass candle holder through which light passes and refracts against the tiles on the wall. The nothing room becomes dazzling, but not overburdened by showiness, just pooling and dripping in warm regality. The queen's room; the angel's kiss marks the stone. Enchantment of this golden hour. I succumb. Something about wintery sundown, and eventual badness of the evening elongates in the extended hours before me. Consideration of anything for too long becomes art. Light on my thigh like the product of stained glass; the churches of my piano days; to be the girl who first basked in the glow of a green window lit behind by the sun.

Art ushers me into realms of feeling that are splattered with color and shape. Each of our evaluations of the thing before us depends on what lay inside, but anything worth looking at will surely remind you of something, which reminds you of something else, which turns the cogs to destabilize brain wave patterns. Beckon to an idea that is new to you. Maybe afterward you'll feel a shift in perspective and gaze toward a new sun. ✦

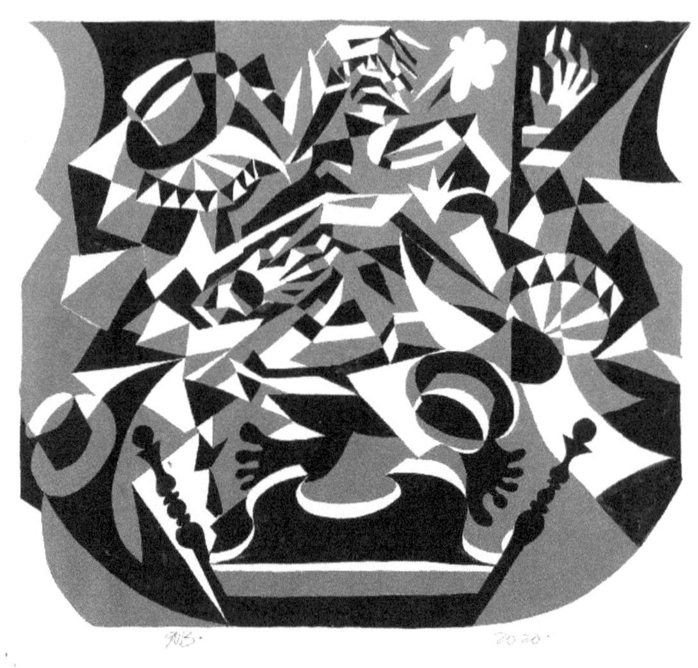

Ryan Bock. *Fever Dream.* 2020. Acrylic on paper. 14 x 17 in. (35.6 x 43.2 cm). Courtesy of the artist

CHAPTER 11

RYAN BOCK'S *FEVER DREAM* IS A SCENE AT THE VERY edge of the corner of disorientation and seduction. It flirts with reality seriously enough to remind of four plague doctors surrounding the death bed, but was bred in the shadowy domain of the artist's mind, recounting his vision which arose during our twenty-first century pandemic. If you want to know how to see through this pinhole to know what the creator knows, you're going to need to think your way into it.

I watched Franz Lang's *Metropolis* for the first time in my early teens. My earliest memory of extended, immersive exposure to German Expressionism. How unable was I to articulate what I felt? I'd never seen those soaring arches and discordant angles together and, in retrospection, I must have been feeling that everything was moving *toward* an indescribable destination—not in the way of the Futurists, via the representation motion and power—achieved through the art of design. Even in dystopia there is impeccable sensibility for a handsome staircase! And then that familiar feeling of learning about something new... a world outside my room, ideas and schools of thought to be plucked and interpreted, and, most importantly, understood. When I was young, I did not often feel that I was swimming within a vaster, fluid course of life. Our life. I'm not sure if what I was experiencing was the optimism of other worlds or the joyous death of loneliness. I had this tingle again when I first read Poe, and then when I saw Giacometti's paintings, when I first heard Ravel, and when my parents would switch on *The Twilight Zone*. Later in college, my film and literary courses sharpened my mind to the language of the horroresque. Experiencing disorientation, fear, uneasiness, and psychological turmoil at the hands of art has brought me great pleasure over the years. Velvet in shades of rouge and lakes of black and silver under sheets of icy fog: a world constantly steeped in the stuff of dark dreams. Because our condition feels unreal to me without more nihilistic interpretations that can be derived from the lowest points of a person's emotions.

I moved from Manhattan to Brooklyn and began meeting new people. One young man immediately ensnared my attention, a painter whose works of black, grey, and white, fractured object and light into nearly unreadable shape. Ryan Bock: painter of the eerie and sculptor of the strange, conjuring products of a mind clearly tormented by *many things*. Great, I thought. Then I was smitten on first sight because he was wickedly striking with elegant mannerisms and the sensibility of a modern goth. Like-minded soul, kindred ghost.

I got involved writing wall text for a forthcoming solo exhibition of his at the wonderful Deep Space Gallery over in New Jersey. A few weeks later he invited me to visit his studio in East Williamsburg. I took a car to the wrong building and then walked over. After finally ar-riving at the space, I was charmed to see that it was not only adorned with an incredible volume of work, but that its walls had been painted in Ryan's shapes and colors as well. Storybookesque, the maker vignetted by his cre-ations. There was young Ki Smith building white frames in Ki Smith uniform, all white, all business, white but-ton-down, slim white pants, and white snake pointy-toed cowboy boots, on the phone in the process of helping to sell a Basquiat painting on the secondary market, or something. He hung up and immediately asked my opin-ion about some artist represented by Gagosian. He said the artist was trash; I like a contrarian (months later, I would help open the brick-and-mortar Ki Smith Gallery in Harlem as editorial director). The commencement of a writer's first real interdisciplinary collaborations.

I told Ryan to free-associate to me about this forthcoming exhibition entitled *The Golem: Objects of Security*, while I took notes. After a little back and forth, I looked around, noticing how some masks he'd created for the jazz musicians *Onyx Collective* were propped on a Bockhaus Staircase in the corner. I'd just interviewed their visual director that week. On the way home that evening, it was all August. I really breathed, and I walked all the way home, golden and in the haze, heat rising from the sidewalk. The shadows of dusk revealed themselves to me: a vine climbing the dilapidated roof of a brownstone or the slender arch of a streetlight's reach upon the pavement. Later that night I was deeply intoxicated in thought. Meaning of text to picture; unutterable moments sparking between two mediums that can never quite by quantified by either practice, thereby reinforcing the unique spirit and necessity of each.

The coming months brought increased productivity for me, as a writer, and a feeling that collaboration was a new and different untapped current for thinking about writing. I think Ryan's work and practice has become inextricable from my own: spooky friend, partner in artistic-political-social-intellectual pursuit, one who has pulled me out of some of the most trying times of my life, including the one that birthed this book you read now. I do not believe in fate or destiny but I do sometimes wonder at the wondrous chain of events that took place that allowed my practice to come into contact with people who can influence my own trajectory so much. It is a gift to have your lane swayed by another and to be able see (and be seen) by someone whose work is inspirational. I'm not telling you all this to be cute: if you understand the relationship between the writer and the subject of her work you are granted both transparency and dimensionality, and many writers understandably don't want to talk about their approach to their "craft." So much of what I produce is either directly or tangentially in conversation with Ryan's work and with other artists like him. Inwardly, I find that my patterns of thinking really do replicate my experience of the world: ideas clash, the things for which I thirst are not the things that might bring me the most happiness, my opinion of myself turns left and right at the same time. It's a love-affair with parts of modernism (which even since this book's inception I am starting to unbelieve): the absurdity of the world.

The shapes that Ryan makes remind me of a very special version of reality, one that I have felt in shadowy moments over the course of my life. Motifs in his work are colors and architectures: palisades and obelisks, monolithic structures, the sense of being at the mercy of a monster, the feeling that one is being closed in on without an escape route, being peered at from around the corner, specter looming over you, the perpetrator and puppets of fascism, the systems that—as the artist says—are implementd to "keep us from questioning." Other, rarer works of Ryan's present reveries laced with elements of the natural world or quiet, folkloric inhabitants. The dark origins of fairytales and fables.

He voices the fabric of a dark and unanswerable, somewhat intrusive, question that asks what can revealed about how humans treat each other when we peer behind the proverbial curtain. The normalization of atrocity, the abstract illusions of freedom, the top down orders that in my lifetime have only been publicly shaken by a recent rise in class consciousness. This question about how far we are willing to go to decimate and stifle human life does not directly stem from the artist's dreamscape, but cannot exist without his hazy memory of it. Crossroads between subconscious—where things make less apparent sense—and the horrible reality. His images are not precisely of our world, but are of course sensed from within it.

On that note, I have always felt that my subconscious—the kingdom of my unwilful construction and orchestration—implicates my life more than I know. I have always felt with undeniable conviction that the unexplainable, indescribable parts of our lives come from within and meet with reality to produce direction in our lives that is completely beyond our control. Ryan and I have both taken note of how dreams operate in film and television, particularly for creative touchstones like Lynch. You could say we're indebted to him. I don't trust any kind of artistic person who doesn't incorporate her favorites into her DNA. You must know the traditions from whence you spiral and navigate…

I have a number of Ryan's works in my apartment. Sometimes I sit on the floor in front of a painting (not just his, anything on my walls) with a glass of wine and a notepad and a quietly streaming Scriabin recording, and indulge myself in recounting the day. The process could transpire over the course of minutes or an hour, never very long. What is important is letting art seduce you into a mental submission, so that you are open to what art tells you.

I want to be ravished by it a little bit, not in some creepy sexy way—I am tired of hypersexualization of aesthetics—but cerebrally. Ryan's *Fever Dream* comes out of a time of unparalleled anxiety and mass hysteria and death and destruction produced by COVID-19 and the deplorable failure of our governmental officials and systems to manage it. Out of all his work, it speaks to me because of how deeply Ryan's mental health has experienced tumult during all of this, and all of those with intense fears of falling sick and of the spread of illness. I've always found that those most tormented by the state of the world around them impulsively feed their empathy and curiosity into what they create. The painting speaks to his ability to continue despite this, to paint to survive. To paint in isolation and let feelings and visions rupture onto the paper.

Fever Dream will one day be a relic; it will outlast this hellishness so that when we look upon it, we are pulled back into the gargantuan and sickening system of late (post?) capitalism that has possibly, for the first time in my own lifetime, began to make itself apparent enough to be detected in the United States not just to academia and the far left but to all; nothing unites us except for the hatred of this losing economic structure. The subject at the heart of the painting's composition is flayed on the bed between four masked doctors. It is not just courage that compels us to face the things that horrify us: it is the understanding that if the grotesque and the traumatizing go unexplained, that they will consume us. Once you catch the longing for art—and I mean visual art, film, literature, fashion, philosophy, physics, everything—you can't stop.

So many of us who feel the urge to create—and of course, also those who might not but who have other means of expression—constantly wonder why, for what, for whom, and to what end? Why bother? But I've been amazed to find that… even in moments that I thought might be the own twilight of my life, Ryan's work has presented itself to me like a carnelian, glowing ember on the edge a rocky shore. It is lapped by a ceaseless and quiet wave, time and time again, and hisses across to me. It is speaking into the wind. But it is the precariousness of the ember's location—its melancholy and oneirity, the fact that it should not in theory exist but does, and that it will always guide my senses to the edge of the water—that lays me into a deep rest, so that when I've decided that the moon will rise again, it may, and I will see it through my blinds, stretch my writing shoulder behind my back, keep my head down as the words, now sensical and ordered, come back to me. ✦

✦   ✦   ✦   ✦   ✦   ✦   ✦   ✦   ✦

THE WORDS OVERTOOK ME WHEN I CEASED CORRALLING them into a beast of my own. Language can be merciless when it remains unshaped. It can be even more merciless when it is seeped into the world with intent to suppress. I think about how language is used for harm at the hands of a person who intends it; racist, a misogynist, a mega-lomaniac, a president—oftentimes the same people who defend their words by saying *it's just their opinion* and *it's not that deep* and *they're just words*. Language and art are the strongest tools of the mind I know.

The writing and art that I love tends to ask a question rather than answer one. It refrains from dogmatism and from the need to impose but comes, rather, from a yearning to impress, to mingle. Good writing holds the reader at its mercy, whether it presents abundance and utopia or the despair of inescapable torture.

All the art and writing in the world—a poem or a PSA or a user's guide to entering the matrix—tells us something about their source. Even the attempt to say nothing expresses something, is sometimes more jarring than the most didactic lecture. Stories that run wild at the hands of a lie grow dangerous. ✦

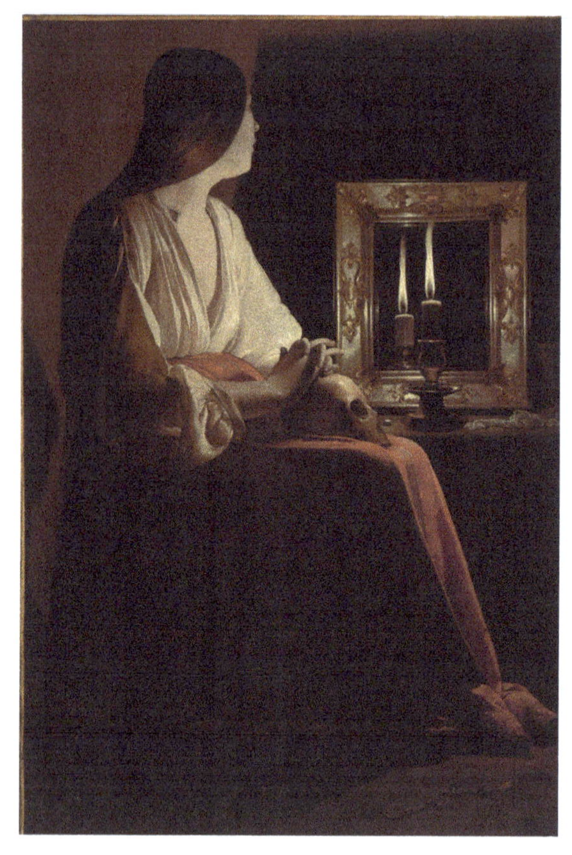

Georges de La Tour. *The Penitent Magdalen.*
ca. 1640. Oil on canvas. 52 1/2 x 40 1/4
in. (133.4 x 102.2 cm). The Metropolitan
Museum of Art, New York. Gift of Mr. and
Mrs. Charles Wrightsman, 1978

CHAPTER 12

I'VE BEEN TRAPPED IN THIS APARTMENT, WAITING TO be provoked, watching my bones embolden Giger-style on my spine when I slouch over in front of the mirror, looking out the window, fearing the figure of a man crouched under the streetlight. Life weaves into the historicized matter of fable. Unreturning to the present. Greying affliction with simultaneous thirst to still mind. It remains dark this morning, late spring full of musky damp and moss on the pathway. Have been alone for months. The rooms grown clean and unadorned. I leave things on the sidewalk in front of my door. I gave my furniture away because they became talismans of the cursed. It seems that just the other day I ground my right palm into the inky black image of the robed and praying lady Mary Magdalene. My fingers were greedy; I wanted to suck the blood from the flesh concealing the soft path into the heart—the great connector—to become one with her image and find a new body more dependable and trainable. Like a horse. I reached toward the saint's expression so full of dolor and knowing. It was warm and sweet. My fingers to corners of the five known features on her face. It hurt; and in the divinity of the moment I closed my eyes, wanting to be everything. Greedy in your quenching, the oxygen left my brain with a whispered "forget this" and the clouds over the night sky kept coasting along with purpose and direction. From above I see my eyes go blank and fizzle away into their sockets. A slate. Two lies. All the atmosphere gone out of me, but nothing was promised.

False as the moment was, it lingered in my apartment for three days plus a half, casting eyes at me. I bathed repeatedly in attempt to cleanse myself of the extraordinary, unattainable want. It had moved beyond my control and turned into a Moloch rearing its head toward the innocent. I thought that a temperature nearly too hot to bear could sweat out the desperation, and I was right. Dipping back in scalding water, you slowly dissipated. I clasp my hands together to imitate the motion of one hoping for reassurance or connection. Maybe it was a plea. To whom? After the seventh submergence, I was fine. Finding five-five-five everywhere I look. What is left for me in this absence? Life in the presence of art means you are never alone.

Hundreds of years of Christianity and its iterations and precursors hung to dry Mary Magdalene's condemned promiscuity, and celebrated lifestyle change, bringing into common belief that she sought repentance after her introduction to Christ. But these claims to her early sins were borne of falsehood; her role of prostitute-turned-pious was just an interpretation of the story (made popular by a pope who confused her with a different woman of the same name who had, in fact, been a lady of the night). "Sin" is juicier and more enjoyable to share. We often adapt stories over the course of time to bend to the popular messages we want to express in any given social atmosphere. That's why the Bible is so fucked up but also an entertaining read (see Revelations), depending on who you are and how you interpret the stories (and what they mean to you). There's no question about how particular tales spread, though. Magdalene became a tool for moral lesson, preached by the unbreakable lineage of popes that continues today under a guise of good-doing and dogs in heaven. The ones in our dear States are busy destroying the critical and social fabric of the country with their sickening agenda, calling the queers "groomers" while the Catholics touch children behind closed doors and get paid for it. A never-ending parade of miserable and wretched figures of Christian monotheism and their impossible god.

Obviously, groups in the margins have traditionally been unable to control depictions of their own sexuality or nonsexuality. The stories just get written. American fleshly pursuits go unquestioned when executed by dominant counterparts both in and outside the dominion of religion. For a non-believer the ways of seeking societal forgiveness aren't guidebooked: keep your sex-life private, tie intimacy to domesticity, treat your body as a temple, pursue romance as the object of adornment and not an equal partner, worry about whether or not you are desired and not about whether or not you desire.

I sometimes feel I am forever entrapped in the histories and patterns of the scriptural Words. The story of Mary as relayed in the foundation of Christian teachings—their bible—actually denotes her as being a powerful figure adorned with the burden of bearing witness. The hallowed Mary Magdalene saw a miracle before her, *"as she stood weeping outside the tomb, and as she wept she stooped to look into the tomb."* That's straight from the pages of the book. In place of Jesus's body: two angels in white. Where is the truth of Mary Magdalene and her visions? Cults of us yearn to know.

French Catholic Baroque La Tour created several versions of Mary Magdalene encased in the same scene with variations in angle and mis-en-scene, which he began in the 1630s, exist in various collections. It is unknown if they were all commissions or if the artist just had an affinity for painting her, but it does point toward the strong religious imagery that dominated La Tour's work as he got older. Kelly Bagdanov has extensively researched Mary Magdalene's legacy and places her as a popular character in the 1600s during the Counter-Reformation, when La Tour was painting. And in her thesis entitled "Sacred Flame: Meditative Mysticism in the Works of Georges de La Tour," Elizabeth Carleton beautifully charts the course of the Magdalene paintings in a beautiful lexicon of midnight language. She describes La Tour's Magdalene: "While Caravaggio introduces us to a human and sympathetic sinner, La Tour shows us a woman spiritually transcending while still maintaining his focus on the humanity of the saint." I too believe this Magdalene exists between here and godliness and brings us somewhere between the two.

The ghostly and powerful *The Penitent Magdalene* on display at The Metropolitan Museum of Art in Manhattan does not stray from the historically-accepted, sexualized, and inaccurate character, as Mary Magdalene prays. La Tour's work was inspired heavily by Caravaggio, and as a fellow bringer-of-light, his scenes glowed in candlelight and were silhouetted in darkness. I've never seen the painting in the quiet and solitude it portrays. Not sure if that's important, but what matters is that the work is beloved and recognizable by a wide audience. The painting must continuously teach or remind those who look upon it of the history it has been prescribed, rather than the one that is biblically accurate. Despite this, what I see here is a woman beholden to something that no one else can see. What is she looking at? The artist has chosen not to adopt a perspective which might show the reflection of her face in the mirror. In fact, it sits below her line of sight. A shunning of vanity? Perhaps... but perhaps the pursuit of something greater. Reflection of the world upon itself. Higher than being shackled to a ruler-god. In writing our own stories we define ourselves.

Yesterday I was asked what part of myself I wanted to kill off in a recent turning point of my life. My friend and I joke about performing hack lobotomies on one another when he gets back from Los Angeles. Icepick up the nose. Parts of the internet find insensitivity in this particular joke. Life would be quite unlivable if our relationships to our own lives weren't allowed to be a little bit of a joke.

I hope that my memories at the end of the world will be significant in shaping who I am, not for others, for myself.

So that when I meet the end I have a full deck of cards and a path into whatever comes next, whether it be eternal silence or something unknown. I have the luxury to prepare.

Mary Magdalene's skin is corpishly white, wordless and bloodsucked. My fingers yearn to become entwined with her image, to gain knowledge via contact. De La Tour paints a skull, a candle, a strand of pearls. Magdalene's hands are clasped, of course. Her hair is placed over her shoulder like a curtain, like the still ocean, contained and tame. The loose garment leaves as much to be desired as any man might want. Her lips are slightly parted—here are some heteronormative (or are they just universal and I'm too 21st century-pilled to see past it?) signals that do not change as the centuries roll by... we watch each other gesture cyclically and fall into infinite and pitiful human-acting loops.

My engagement with art is beholden to historical meanings and doting upon my own interpretations, and if my own interpretations come with a bit of correctional history... it's okay with me. All you have to do is scan the web for her name and you will find that I'm right. Perhaps you already knew. Perhaps my practice here is just delusional self-correction. Perhaps you already know. The essence of what I write is self-indulgence anyway.

Mary Magdalene stares above the reflection of herself in the mirror, toward a place that the viewer cannot see. A dark corner of the room. Crepuscular silence. Symbol of eternity. Vision of agency delicately slipping away. What is she seeing? Probably there is nothing there.

I am asphyxiated even just to think of you as I write this. And distantly angry but it comes back with ease. And moments later I didn't want to move my teeth from the sinewy muscle. I chewed into the tattoo Mary Magdelene and tasted the metallic flavor of blood on my tongue. I wanted to cause more harm. *Are you supposed to get saints tattooed, isn't it some kind of sin?* Stupid thing to be wrongful for. I freed her, anyway. There is the idea of the woman Mary Magdelene and the art, the meaning of the art and the inky, fleshy representation divorced from any real meaning, and finally there is the person she thought she was. Of course the latter is rarely perceived. Perhaps better to be left behind altogether than to be told who you were. *I'm sorry I can't ask you.*

We paint such grand horizons in our solitude. It was the illusion of an interlude to my days in which I—in the interest of bliss and love—stopped conversing with myself for just a moment. ✦

+   +   +   +   +   +   +   +   +

MY THOUGHTS... THEY RETURN TO *YOU*, NOT *YOU* A person but *you* an idea. I'm only ever alone with *you*, the divine magnum opus I've orchestrated in my head, the story of my life. *You*, what I come back to, all I have. Me. I do not have a self in the way that some have an identity, but what I have is *you*. I want to seduce *you* out of yourself and flay *you* upon the page. Strike a match until your crimson bleeds from the paper. The candle burns with definition, melting away its waxy, fat sustenance. I am corralling the words that will compose this unnamed thing. That is why I am writing this. I'm trying to account for pain and loss, to reshape it through language toward complexity and nuance, I drag my hands across the stoney walls in search of the exit. +

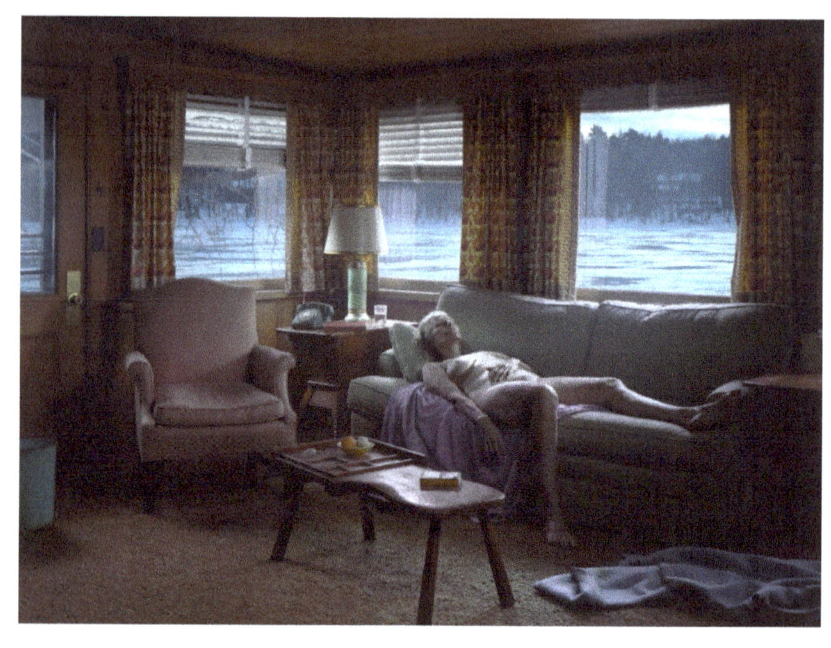

Gregory Crewdson. *Reclining Woman on Sofa.*
2014. Digital pigment print. 37 ½ x 50 in.
(95.3 x 127 cm). Gagosian Gallery, New York

CHAPTER 13

THE MESSINESS OF MY MIND HAS ONLY BECOME MORE pronounced as years and their memories accumulate. My ability to thread a cohesive narrative or to focus on a singular topic can't parallel so many other writers I admire and I am sure you can tell by the writing here that I don't really want to find harmony and cohesion anyway. Though I do think of thickly-paged volumes that recount the loss of a great love, for example, or the story of the rise and fall of a family, and long for the ability to engage my writing in an extended journey. People often describe writers as having a gift for storytelling; I am not one of those. The isolation of a memory feels burdensome. It makes me sad. I always had camcorders and point-and-shoots growing up. I thought of taking pictures as a way of recording life, the way I write in a journal or press flowers between parchment paper: to prove that something happened. Those fragments of life were lost in the web, crashing down with the final blows to Geocities, MySpace, you know... the material has to exist outside my mind for me to really remember what it was like to be on the internet frontier.

When I was an undergraduate studying at Syracuse, right near the end of those internet-y times, a peer asked me to play subject in a series of pictures she wanted to take: the assignment was to emulate a famous photographer. The crew drove me out to an empty parking lot that was as ice-ridden as any given road upstate. In the night, I knelt down into the snow, looking into construction lights positioned from beyond the camera's frame. She kept directing me to drain my facial expression of emotion. To let my arms dangle.

Upon first seeing Gregory Crewdson's photographs that day after modeling, I thought they looked more like paintings than real images. I was flabbergasted. I'd never seen anything like it and had not had real exposure to contemporary photography, beyond photojournalism, before. Must have been around nineteen at the time. I was shocked by a single frame's capacity to operate like a short story. They seemed cinematic; I read around and found that he was extremely polarizing for critics and curators alike. His two series Twilight (2000) and Beneath the Roses (2005) are probably a couple of his most recognizable. In most photographs, it is clear that *something* is wrong, and one can often pinpoint what it is. A first impression of his work might look something like this: he encompasses Lynch's not-quite-right suburb, Hitchcock's suspended dread, Hopper's postured characters. He himself has mentioned these fellows as his greatest influences, but the viewer might surmise it. He operates in small towns, depicting the lives of the people who live there and the landscapes. The places he captures are postindustrial. Remnants of factories and older technology permeate.

His houses are adorned with simple furniture and minimal pizzazz. More interestingly, they feel outdated by at least a decade. A rectangle of carpet has been removed, and a man stands staring into a massive hole in the ground of his bedroom floor. A faint light shines up from somewhere below the floorboards, from holes or cracks. Dirt and grass and flower spill from the trunk of a car in the middle of the cul-de-sac. Crop circles and a dead woman floating in the flooded living room. Everyone is lonely. Even together they are isolated. These moments are private, come out of necessity, desperation. There is nothing more to be said for these people. This has been happening, I've just walked in on it now, although I suspect I'm on the verge of becoming part of a secret too heavy for me to bear alone. But who would believe me?

Both wonder and dread are present in this question. I wasn't entirely shocked when I learned that Crewdson's father was a psychoanalyst who held his practice in the family's Brooklyn brownstone. Crewdson's own work is deft at provoking our anxieties, at probing unexplained crevices of human psychology and what we envision to be elemental structures of the subconscious.

In winter 2016, I went to the opening night of his newest series *Cathedral of the Pines* at Gagosian. When I look back at my original writing on the subject, I am charmed to see how completely uncharted the visual art landscape of New York City was to me. I was so stunned by his presence and by the celebrity of the City, by the clientele of Gagosian and that Wes Anderson was somewhere in the crowd. And as much as I yearn to temper certain elements of the criticism I think an earlier version of me deserves to live here as well…

In *Cathedral*, Crewdson departs the suburbs and enters the Appalachian Trails outside the Berkshires, in Massachusetts, where he now lives. Nature is more present than ever. He still captures landscapes that dwarf the subjects, the insides of quiet homes, nudity, people sitting in their beds and on their couches. Doing nothing. But, now, his stories don't belong to another universe. The moments captured in these photographs all belong to the quotidian human experience; they are not fantastical. Crewdson takes the elements of his work that initially attracted me to them and engrains them so heavily in the work as to render them nearly unnoticeable. The impression is immediate and sweeping. His older works are still being emulated, but he's moved on.

In one of my favorite photographs from the series, numbered *10*, an old woman sprawls on a couch in a room where the two walls we see are lined with thin windows. Through the glass the lake is frozen, and it seems cold inside, too, a bluish light on the interior in variations of sienna. The last sunlight of the day illuminates the woman's forehead, the gentle slopes of her body. If you look very closely, the chair to her side has the outline of someone just having sat there, or perhaps someone was sitting there every day for many years. Either way, that person is absent here, and I am haunted by it. I think about the woman's nakedness – his subjects often are unclothed – and maybe know what it's like to be her, because it often feels like unclothing oneself is the proper thing to do. I'm sure it can be a sign of defeat, but it is also an act done in comfort. There's a door to the left with a window and no curtain, although I suspect no one will be arriving here any time soon. It could be that the pain has just begun. But maybe this is what it looks like to achieve peace after a long time deprived of it.

Later on, I learned that Crewdson had sat in that armchair to give his model directions. Upon standing, he liked the indent he'd left and kept it. I had a dream about Crewdson two nights ago, which happened to be the eve of his birthday. I'm thinking about his artistry so continuously; it's not just a coincidence.

I had never considered the encapsulation of the singular moment in art until I met his work. I still always feel I'm writing *around* something rather than getting at it directly. I worry that to be frank is to be cute, or that to be direct is to place too little agency in the hands of the reader. Crewdson has discussed how his work attempts to capture "the dynamic between beauty and sadness that we experience continuously." I believe, now in my life more than ever, that what we create is often more beautiful than our experience of it.

I keep saying to myself that I don't like a feel-good story; so much of the pop-culture and literature we consume as a people resolves itself so neatly. It attempts to create a universal pre-packaged, feel-good language that prescribes rather than prompts imagination. Maybe it feels like a flattening of reality, an erasure of subtext, or maybe it even has something to do with my own fear of losing touch with the world around me by being lulled into a passive happiness. It is inconceivable to me that a moment—even one of divine happiness or despair—can be void of complexity. The extremes only exist because they are in opposition. We have to tuck our secrets into our work; the trajectory of our lives culminates in each new thing we create. I suppose I hadn't noticed it at first—the changes taking place in Crewdson's works—because I consumed his practice all at once, devouring any photos I could find online, searching for variety, for new images I hadn't seen before. I began collecting his books out of order, and perhaps that wouldn't matter to someone else. Now that I've caught up, I have time to synthesize and wait and see. This is the difference, to me, between considering the art of the dead and the art of the living. Wanting to parallel your artistic growth to the time and conditions in which you create.

Cathedral of the Pines is the occasion on which Crewdson encounters himself, on which Lynch and Hopper and Hitchcock become part of his DNA rather than bulkier components of the photographs. Oddities in his work have gone into hiding, rendering the work more unclassifiable. I have a strong conviction that this series is suspended not in horror but in possibility. It reminds me of the title of that Flannery O'Connor story; it's as if everything that rises must converge. I don't assume that the moment after the one portrayed will be worse, I just assume that this precise moment is pivotal. There would be no way for me to catch these instances as they occur in my own life. I recount them later, even if just seconds later. It's more significant to me that I know these moments *can* be realized; I think there is a kindness, a forgiveness, that is very quiet, but that is, really, the undercurrent of every experience I've had looking at those photographs. ✦

✦ ✦ ✦ ✦ ✦ ✦ ✦ ✦ ✦

OUTSIDE THE DIVINE MAGNUM OPUS OF DREAMS AND visions and delusions of the sacred world in the safety of my mind , there are reasons to embrace life: the people, the things they make, the ways they tend to want to show why they are special through miniscule gestures like a manner of entering the staircase or turning the page of their book. The way the music they love is fiercely held by them, the movie *they knew first* becomes a war cry. People are always expressing reasons to live. And within their sweet constructions: The symbolic changing of the seasons, the cyclical nature of our years on Earth. The idea that each moment is one of change and is therefore full of possibility. No need to look down the road. A future doesn't exist for you, even, unless you pave it. And here I am now wanting so desperately to stay.

More important than telling ourselves stories in order to live is constructing our own truths as we experience life. Figuring out why we are the way we are; introspecting and sipping the blood of our years on earth. ✦

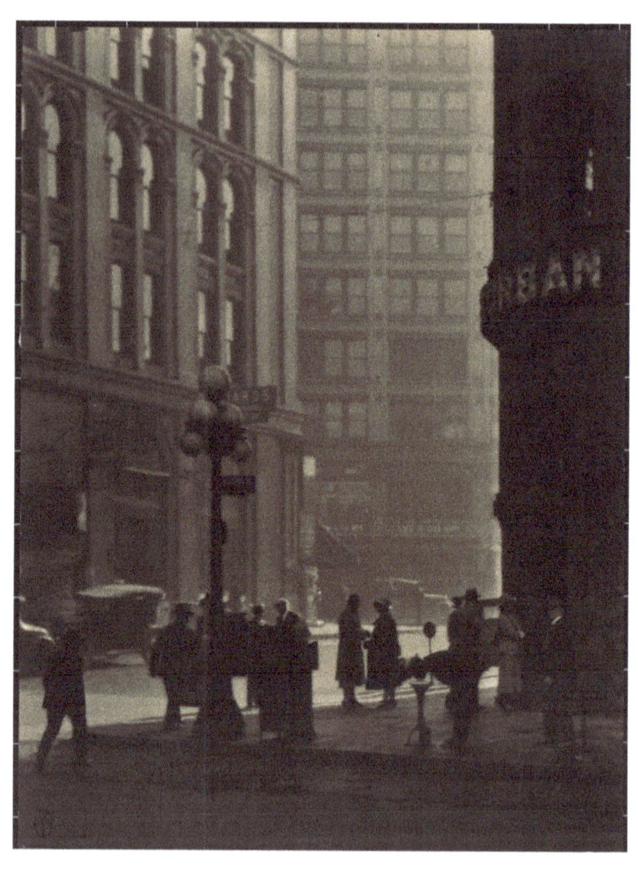

Yukio Morinaga (1888–1968). Canyon of Streets.
C. 1925. Gelatin silver print. 13 3/8 x 10 1/8 in.
(34 x 25.7 cm). Randall Family Collection

CHAPTER 14

Have I mentioned where I'm from? A rush of memory bathed in emerald and jade. The Pacific Northwest Coast. The Ring of Fire, waiting for The Big One. The ecology: our tampering with it, its diversity, how the glaciers and volcanoes are background to the perennial greenest green you might ever see, and how the systems of natural water trickle down from the peaks to Puget Sound or further off to the ocean. Deep time veins. You could follow them—I've wanted to—and find your way to the Pacific shoreline. Fog settling into the pines. Dishonored treaties, missionaries, canning factories, rogue anarchists, communes, Chief Seattle's (siʔaɬ) grave along the shoreline of the Salish Sea. Manifest Destiny damming up the waterways.

But I love the tiger lilies and their recurved petals. We used to snowshoe through the Cascades in the winter. I walked through my grandparents' farm one last time before it left the family forever. I'd kneel to harvest lavender, rhubarb, pluck salmonberries in the forest behind my childhood home. Used to sit in the monkey tree by the beach with my grandmother. I always liked to hike across a sturdy bridge. When I was older, I made pilgrimages to Raymond Carver's grave: the Northwest is Carver Country. Everything back there that I remember is surrounded by a golden halo of light, like a pinhole camera of the divine.

It was all so quiet. My life was small and still completely mine. I was not a child of poverty or of exorbitant wealth, of lavishness or dearth. Only of so much love to overshadow the terrible things that had happened and with my face buried in the meadow's grass. Time alone. I loved to walk outside in the summer. I lean forward and inhale until I remember a time when solitude and isolation were expected in a forest tall enough to be seemingly older than time.

The first six years of my inhabitance on the East Coast were filled with longing for home. I'd dedicated my research for school to the political and ecological history of the Pacific Northwest. The recent facts of colonization and of the land had never been documented well enough, deserve to be told and retold as history grows uncovered and corrected. By the end of my graduate program, I found disconnect between what I wrote and how I felt, a sense of being an outsider and looking in. I'd slowly dismantled my life back West and rebuilt it in New York. By then, writing from memory made the prose fall flat. My hands weren't in the earth, so I was unable to reconstruct the memories of walks through the mountains or across the meadows. There were two bookshelves in the Butler Library stacks dedicated to Washington State. I'd pored over them enough to know that all that I didn't know couldn't be found out from twenty-five hundred miles away. It was quiet in the stacks' cage late at night and I would think about my inability to execute groundwork in the process of researching. A lot of my essays were set in tying local ecological change to my personal experiences growing up in the region. It felt somehow shameful. Perhaps a text of this sort's ability to transcend its reader depended on its proximity to its source. It collected too much detritus as it coursed through my life, losing the clarity and color it needed to remind of a real place and time.

I mourn my own inarticulateness of that subject now because the subject of climate change is more public than ever. The corporations have been greenwashed, the term "greenwashed" has even entered our public discourse, the influencers are nearly done buzzwording the term and making it their personal cause. Tiktokkers throw invasive or monocultural wildflower species into the soil of a incinerated forest. Strange children crop up as the faces of environmental awareness. Perhaps I've lost the right to that material forever.

The experiences of art back around the Salish Sea have been quiet, self-reflective, exploratory. No flashiness. No friends, no booze, no crowds, no asking to be reviewed or asking for a review. The Cascadia Art Museum sits in a mid-century low, curved roof building right off the ferry docks in Edmonds. I heard it used to be a bingo hall. Recently I went there and saw an exhibition of photographs by Shedrich Williames and paintings by Leo Kenney; a beautiful pairing. One summer I saw an exhibition of botanically fixated works. Another summer I saw the pictures of the Japanese American photographer Yukio Morinaga and simultaneously picked up *Shadows of a Fleeting World*, by David F. Martin and Nicolette Bromberg, an invaluable book documenting the Seattle Camera Club and its members. Morinaga was a Pictorialist, meaning that his works were less documentary and more filled with soft-edge and based on the emotional projection of the person behind the lens. They recall the otherworldliness of silent film sets. Frozen time, material drama, life as a long poem, life as the grass beneath a leafy tree in flux of shadow and light.

Morinaga was Issei, a first-generation immigrant to the country. The influx of Asian immigrants during the building of the United States' railroad system brought anxiety and anger amongst the European colonizers (working and ruling class), resulting in rampant xenophobia and ensuing violence against the entire Asian community in the States. The government's implementation of laws such as the Chinese Exclusion Act (1882) only catalyzed public expressions of hatred toward the community. By the time WWII devastated the globe, heightened racism targeting Asian Americans would have come as no surprise.

In Seattle, a small and vibrant organization called the Seattle Camera Club was founded by Japanese photographers. It thrived during the 1920s until declining after the depression, and eventually ending with the attack on Pearl Harbor. Morinaga was a member of the SCC. His photographs often captured the urban streets or people at work, making him unique within the larger body of photographers who often preferred landscapes of wildlife or flowers or abstract portraiture—even today, the Pacific Northwest region of the United States is ripe for nature photographers, for hikers and extreme athletes who climb to the snowy tops of the Cascades or Olympics to show the rest of us something we might never see.

Photographers sit, watch, breathe meaning into what they see. They *capture*; they immortalize life on Earth and feed our need to revisit ourselves. They let life pass *into* them rather than *by* them.

Morinaga's photographs of downtown Seattle are delicate and emotional, populated by hazy and ghostlike silhouettes of silent streetgoers on their way to somewhere. *Canyon of Streets* (c. 1925) is not, perhaps, Morinaga's most celebrated work. There might be others more beautiful, or make a stronger statement. But *Canyon* is one of my favorites, because the right side of the photograph glows in a radiant ribbon of light, defining the dark building that casts the foreground in blackness. The light that enters the frame of his photograph comes from an unseen place down the avenue and casts down the pavement, and in that way, it makes a promise to the viewer, telling you that the coming and going of warmth is inevitable. Cities do that, don't they? They give and take away the middle of the afternoon. They'll chill your bones in shadow for two blocks, and you'll close your jacket and speed your stride, before allowing the sky to open upon you. Again, feeling your own body. It's like the story about the wind and sun in competition to blow off a man's jacket. You become the subject of a story when you walk across a city. All is yours to see and you are surrounded. And you are so small. I think Morinaga knew that. His early works… they come with a narrative, expressing the strange paradox of a new and growing Seattle where the recession of the timberline unfurls in slow-time and the buzz of new commerce still soars. He photographed shipyard workers and fisherman and trains billowing with smoke, a clear eye for the propelling forces of the city. In another photograph, the person behind the camera—and by extension, the viewer—looks out to dock pilings. Beyond that, there is a clearing in the sky and a tugboat returns to the harbor.

After Executive Order 9066 declared the removal and internment of Japanese Americans, Morinaga was detained and interned in Minidoka in Idaho, along with over 9,000 people. Morinaga had moved to the country when he was only a teenager, had worked a number of odd jobs and had forged friendships that would last him a lifetime. Decades of life thrown into disarray because of a global war beyond his direct engagement or control. When he was allowed to return to Washington, David F. Martin writes that "In an act of defiance toward the government that had betrayed him Morinaga refused to pay any more taxes." Years later he starved himself.

I don't relay this detail of his life to create a sense of melodrama—though this singular career could never be overshadowed by a writer hoping to spin a story of his personal affairs —but to add a drop of evidence into our ocean of existing knowledge that tells us that the powerful ones and their belongings—including military and agricultural-industrial complexes, mass incarceration and its slave labor, and now technofascism—choke the possibility for art by its throat.

Morinaga was exhibiting his work internationally by the time the government misidentified him as an enemy of the state. And to think that his practice must have been shattered during his years at Minidoka. The equipment and conditions that would have been necessary for him to produce photographs would have been essentially impossible, given the documentation of the resources available in the country's ten internment camps. Having been broken, the artist lost his way. An incalculable loss.

What Morinaga's work did so wonderfully was suggest the continuation of humanity within an increasingly mechanized world. People felt alienated by the new technologies around them, including the indigenous communities who'd gotten along with their own innovations and who often saw no return on any investment in government projects, and even the farmers who saw themselves increasingly replaced by machines with no incentivization for the future. The cities that towered over everyone's heads were—and still are—a reminder at once of both corporeal insignificance and human creation. These sleek devices cannot exist without us, in fact exist for us, are made understandable by us, are the products of us. Morinaga's body of work feels to me like friend's firm and fleshy massage right under my shoulder blade. Sometimes my body gets tense without me knowing it. I'll let a friend or a professional dig into my back. Afterwards, I feel no sense of distortion, only a slow return to my body's harmony. Planes on their way across the Pacific, overtaking the low-hung rainclouds, breaching the threshold. Three men on a raft, rolling paint onto the side of a windwhipped building. A person in a hat traversing the cobblestoned street in the shade of an otherwise sunny afternoon. ✦

✦   ✦   ✦   ✦   ✦   ✦   ✦   ✦   ✦

THERE ARE SO MANY REASONS PEOPLE FEEL CONNECTED to each other and to the Earth and our galaxy and the matter and antimatter we slowly discover that expands and collapses beyond. I've mentioned that like so many of us, I love the changing of the seasons. Emotional stagnancy pervades the arrival and settling-in of trauma and sadness, which course through everyone's veins at least a little. I want the promise of renewal without the commitment of stasis: to be born over and over again. Each time I walk through my apartment's front door: new leaf, stray cat under the hot moonlight, snail on the wet wall, fall of snow tempering the noise from the street. Feels like an offering being brought to me; all I have to do is observe. *A day at a time.* ✦

144

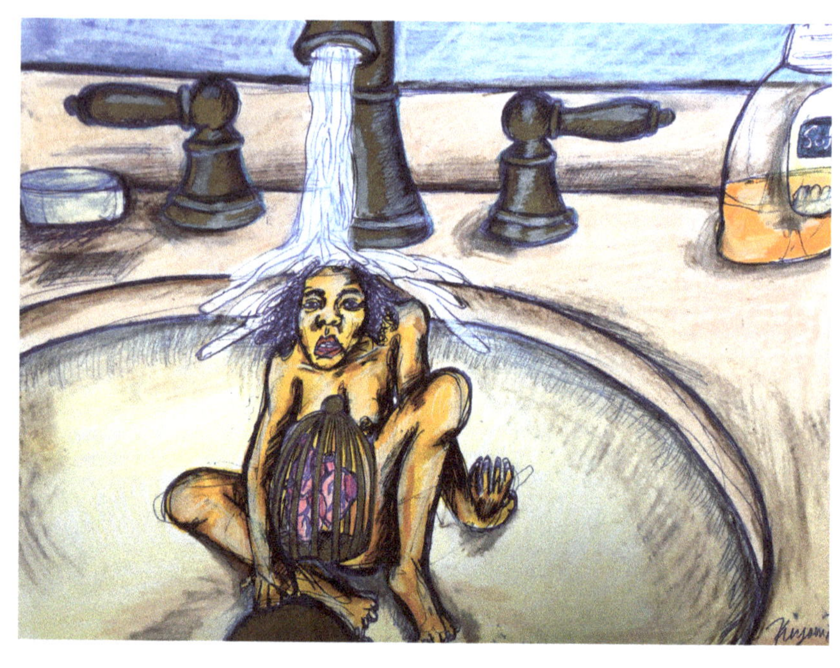

Kiyomi Taylor. *Problems of Feeling II (Sink).* 2020. Ink and colored pencil on paper. 10 x 13 ¼ in. (25.4 x 33.7 cm). Courtesy Ki Smith Gallery

CHAPTER 15

Kɪʏᴏᴍɪ Tᴀʏʟᴏʀ ᴅʀᴇᴡ ᴛʜʀᴇᴇ ᴘɪᴇᴄᴇs ꜰᴏʀ Kɪ Sᴍɪᴛʜ Gallery as part of a group exhibition of works on paper, at the beginning of the pandemic in 2020. I was the editorial director of the gallery at the time, and our hope in putting together a body of affordable, easily-hangable artworks was that our community could bring something full of meaning and wonder into their homes, which they'd be seeing so much of for the coming years. I oversaw the production, design, and writing related to the gallery's exhibition catalogues, press releases, wall texts, and other written documents, all which focused on trying to generate entry points for our friends, communities, enemies, lovers to understand the work and artist on display.

I was excited about this odd show which reconnected us to our people during a time of such extreme isolation and—for those of us stuck at home—emphasis on self-growth. People were learning to bake and knit and produce music.

Outside the city, they tended gardens and made their sheds into artist studios.

Out of all the work we received from our artists, Kiyomi's trio of drawings affected me the most. I'd worked with her once before on a group show and was attracted to the narrative-biographical elements of her work being treated as these huge cultural monuments. I also loved how her introspection bled from the work into the room it inhabited with such integrity for personal feeling. The artist has expressed how she often depicts iterations of the self in her work, one of which appears here in the sink's basin under running water. Taylor's palette has this 1980s electricity, which, in this drawing is bolstered by the blue ballpoint pen and its slight, chemical translucence. The materials feel so apt given the circumstances of their creation. The work adopts an overall opulence not generally granted by this pen's special texture and hue. This ballpoint blue composes the majority of the linework and shading in the drawing. Very unusual! It's a pen that reminds me of documents and formalities, of bureaucratic oppression, of being told what to wear, the grind, of corporate passive aggression, of the bruised color that appears on my palm if I write with my left hand: all things that bind us to life rather than ground us in it. But in this work, the medium is so unburdened of all that; it sings a new song.

Although she tends to be a representational artist, she doesn't portray easy narrative. Taylor's practice is often inspired by her own family's complex identities. Taylor intertwines archival family photographs with old television shows like Jurassic Park. Her landscape backdrops are epic and sometimes lush, places of an ancient or perhaps just undiscovered world we cannot access or know as beings of the Anthropocene. There's so much going on, and I can never quite tell if what she's painting is happening in the morning or at dusk; the specificity of a moment seems less important than its grander impact. Context is not given to the viewer but discovered by them. This disorientation is what keeps drawing me to Taylor.

The work mentioned here escapes some of the more dramatic sensory and textured elements—she has lots of fabrics and other materials on her canvases and has executed a handful of installations—that are characteristic of what Taylor tends to incorporate in her work, but it is as fantastical as her larger oeuvre. Her memoirish worldbuilding.

In *Problems of Feeling*, the full-blast sink cleansing doesn't seem to bring catharsis resonates inside me. Something torturous takes place within the domestic realm. When I read the work it tells me that nonsensicality cannot exist because there is already no order to this world. As the title suggests, feeling is not far away but is unreachable, a trio of encaged hearts—the three of hearts in cartomancy generally having connotations of movement, often pointing toward fulfilled creativity or uncertainty or working toward resolve.

I always think about the charts they put up in elementary schools that match a face to a corresponding emotion: a smile signifies happiness, crying signifies sadness, and so on. I suppose they gage how nicely you'll play with others based on your ability to match the emotion to a face. I like these charts because lack of emotional understanding and growth in America has stunted masculinity. At the same time, we grow to learn that emotion is worn differently in different cultures and by different kinds of people. Maybe we should make new charts for adults.

Problems of Feeling seems to confront a personal problem within a larger, uncontrollable structure, endless stream of the faucet beating down on you while you *figure it out*.

If you think about it for a moment, it kind of flashes before your eyes: *should find a career that will make us rich; we should work five days a week; find a mate; consider children; read the* Times; *abide by bipartisan politics; reject radicalism; invest in stocks until we are wealthy enough to retire and more than anything we should suppress our emotions, especially in front of others; do things because they are taught to us and not because we have been given the tools to discover for ourselves. A sophomoric critique of society but it's not wrong! This is done in the name of security and a very British concept of self-preservation, born of churchiness. I admit that perhaps elements of these routines are passed from one generation to the next in hopes that we do not flounder in the face of a pre-existing and rigid societal structure. But these expectations we're taught as children do not pan out so as adults, we identify our confusion as insanity. I've never wanted children, but I'm sure I'll have them. Just depends on the day, and my mood. I assume if they come along I will love them. Hypothetically, I do not. My mom said she also waffled about kids. If I had a child now, I would need to abort it to save myself. I hope the Christians come for me so I can experience their love. Even trying to navigate the confusion here is like a mind game because I'm not sure who these thoughts will offend. I find it funny but I find it dually depressing and usually I'm not even trying to fight. We're not taught to navigate chaos or to interpret chaos. We're supposed to avoid it. I often feel language can't express this sentiment enough and that my attempts to say what I mean will always stop short. Art sometimes picks up where we leave off. Some poets let their language fall apart to bring the inside of their hearts outside. My own prose wanders too much; I drag the blood across the page. Perhaps the writing will get better with experience. I think… I will be better once I cage my heart from seeking solace in order. Trying to live up to my idea of what a life should be as defined by the majority has brought its share of disappointment.*

Because I know this to be true, I now live with a constant suspicion that something is just slightly wrong all the time. I'm not saying I live in a nightmare. Let me explain it like this: I sense the uncanniness of a dream in my waking hours. Each July-August of the recent years of my life I have felt the calamity of every possible universe melt together underneath my feet and sink me into oblivion. Not sure why it's a summer thing. I looked at the sky on the beach the other night and felt it bending around me and felt that my eyes were lighting the sky and did not feel that I was the one perceiving something already lit. Is it possible that I orchestrate my life? When I close my eyes it ceases to exist. Open them again and I remember that my feet are in the sand. I stood for a little while with my hands behind my head and then I climbed the lifeguard's chair and lay sprawled across the footrest. I bent my head backwards over the wood panels and felt seawater rush to the tips of my hair. Things made as much sense upside down. I thought a plastic bag was a crab. And then the earth turned a little more and unclothed the sun over on the horizon. The story doesn't end there; it doesn't end anywhere.

It's a *Problem of Feeling*, as Kiyomi Taylor says. In her paintings, the character is fighting for her life, alone. What happens to her is unwitnessed except by me as I stand in their presence. I love Taylor's impulse for strong and deranged confrontation of her own psyche. It's inspiring, because otherwise, the hot girls of my generation have caricatured their need for a year of rest and relaxation (no shade) so much that it has come full circle and I see them swallowing their pain in exchange for what? Following pin-brained internet dudes into the White Supremacy pipeline. Becoming actually hateful and bland. Wanting so desperately to be cool and romanticizing how much they lose touch with themselves. The 2020s whisper that they want more…

I will plunge myself into every feeling. The sky is calming because it is shapeless. When we write we like to pause; we think we will create drama or suspension. Seems like the natural place… to leave off at the beginning of a new day. ✦

✦   ✦   ✦   ✦   ✦   ✦   ✦   ✦   ✦

And so we can break out of the stasis of our hopelessness on our own. In my childhood when I faced a young rejection of God, I wanted to believe in (or perhaps leech onto) different things: the characters in the stories I read and films I watched, in the musicians I listened to, eventually in myself to figure it all out. And later: in the power of literature and art and music to change the landscape of the human mind, of education to bring disparate minds into contact, of friendship and love to pattern my days. The bond between artmakers and their craft is so strong that it withstands all conditions (you've seen it in my descriptions of artists on these pages); people express themselves even in the most grim and extreme environments, with no tools and with little to no hope. And those artists blissfully brewed in infinite free time also use it to create. Art is always wondering why these inequalities exist; art questions the building blocks of our society; it shows us that we cannot be torn apart. ✦

154

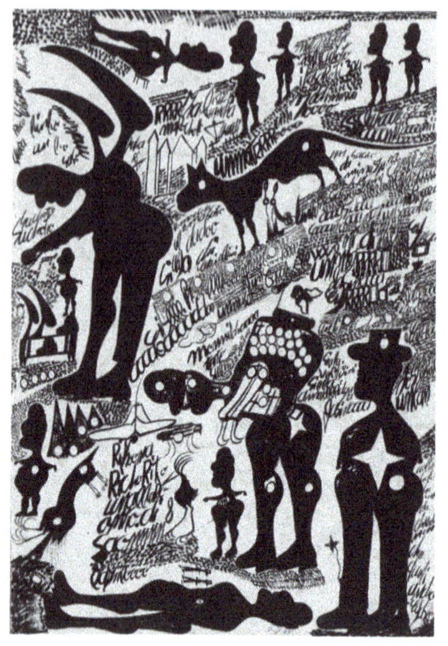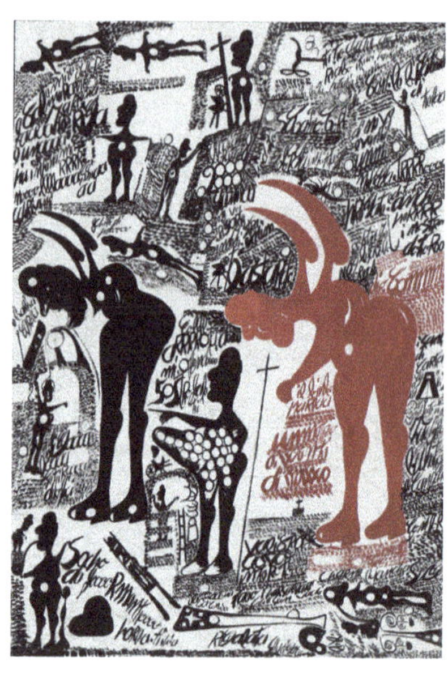

Carlo Zinelli, Untitled, 1968. Gouache
on paper, 27 9/16 x 19 11/16 in. (70 x 50 cm).
Collection de l'Art Brut, Lausanne

CHAPTER 16

THE ENGLISH-SPEAKING ART WORLD USES THE TERM "outsider art" or "raw" or "brut" to describe work created by any individual or group without an institutional, formal art education. I find these categorizations useful in a limited capacity (and otherwise find most categories to be difficult to swallow), so I ignore them unless I am having an in-person discussion about art (during which, the possibility of pigeonholing is less likely than it might be in any written account of my own observations where I feel the need to overexplain and tangent to death). If I could recontextualize the term I would say that it describes a movement of art that spans time, indicating that art is always happening on the peripheries of institutions, that those who haven't been matriculated and hung out to dry by the bureaucratic demands of universities and boards and banalities (I am not excluding myself) might achieve the consideration and recognition of any given viewer. I came into being an appreciator of the art world from a strange angle, myself. I still feel like an onlooker.

Large gallery openings are spectacles and have some Hollywoodesque function very unrelated to 1) enjoying the work and 2) selling the work (of course, the Big Ones sell out before the show opens, even in this economy).

The American Folk Art Museum in New York City showcased a solo exhibition of work by Carlo Zinelli, curated by Valérie Rousseau, in 2017. I hadn't heard of him before, and I thought that the Museum did a nice job at describing the artist and his work, at least by my own standards which means that I could understand everything without having to search for definitions of International Art English on the web. Although they discussed his mental trials and hardships, they avoided sensationalizing the particularities of his behavior and impulses. I hate the glamorization of this as much as I hate celebrity, for different reasons but with the same gusto nonetheless. If you read his brief Wikipedia article, the first sentence is: "Carlo Zinelli (July 2, 1916–January 27, 1974) was an outsider artist who suffered from schizophrenia." [Accessed August 8, 2020]

It feels important to me to re-document here some history on the artist because he is so scantily available to, at least, an English-speaking audience. Zinelli grew up in northern Italy's Verona before being summoned for military service, where he'd remain for five years, some of which were spent fighting as a volunteer for the Spanish front at the end of the Civil War. He began exhibiting some inconsistent behavioral patterns near the end of his tenure, which bled into his civilian life and led to his eventual and permanent residency at San Giacomo alla Tomba hospital back in Verona. It was there that he created the thousands of works on paper (and a handful of sculptures) that are now discussed, exhibited, and archived. A few main factors allowed for these decades of creation that might otherwise be anomalous for any person subjected to the multifaceted atrocities of mental care that took place during the majority of the twentieth century: the artist studio and leadership of the sculptor Michael Noble and the care of several doctors who encouraged Zinelli's artistic growth. The studio implemented at San Giacomo was open nine hours a day and it is reported that Zinelli spent the majority of his time there.

These details and others I know from the wonderful academic work of, particularly, the authors of *Carlo Zinelli: Recto Verso* (2019), published by Collection de L'Art Brut, who holds his archive. He loved to sing and dive into the water. After slowly losing his use of the Italian language after the war, he began to speak his own. Some photographs of him reveal a stylish man. He was devoted to creating and because he was so prolific, he has left behind a massive library of work. The extraordinary *volume* of work acts as somewhat of a roadmap that shows when he introduced certain tendencies or characters or themes into his art.

One telltale characteristic of his paintings is his dense population of both sides of the page with silhouetted characters and patterns. He renders humanlike forms in all variations of positions and with all sorts of bodies: bulgy-jointed, stooped, long-legged, wearing hats, holding canes, laying down, or in procession. There are fantastically elongated crosses that vex the page alongside animals or the machinations of war.

What I find most fascinating about his work is its incorporation of written language. It fills the space in his earlier works, plugging gaps and bending or elongating to surround more significant symbols on the page. Practical and atmospheric tool of sorts, adjusting itself where needed. Later on, it becomes slightly unbridled, composing great oceans of space and moving without regard to the space around it. It becomes, in my possibly idealizing opinion, more central to the work. In the aforementioned Zinelli monograph, Marta Spagnolello speaks in detail about the contents of the artist's language, which ranges from the culinary to the religious to the familial. I am touched by the poetic aspects of the work, of course. In one work, Spagnolello finds "naStela sofiaaaa del para dizo (una stella soffia dal paradiso/a star's breath from paradise)."

I think often about how, societally, we take our relationship to language for granted, highlighting it most often in moments of political unrest, when we realize we are being deceived by, for example, the politician-media complex.

This is a good thing that we do: we must have clarity and truth, and if truth does not exist, then we must at least be given as many details of a story as possible to decide for ourselves what took place. But the other, more abstract applications of language—like poetry—mystifies and beckons. Our brains cue pattern recognition to see order or something familiar in language. A disruption alerts us to its nuances and hues. Sometimes I imagine watching Zinelli at work. For some reason I see him working with his body pressed close to the page with an unbreakable focus. His obsession with making artwork: why? Driven by what?

Seeing repetition within an artistic practice reminds of other kinds of mental repetitions that block the flow of thoughts, productive or otherwise. Perhaps a song gets stuck in your head—very low stakes. Or you keep envisioning a scenario as if you are moments away from being unable to keep it from happening: we're calling these intrusive thoughts at the moment (we joke on Tik-Tok about the intrusive thought of putting a hand on a hot stove or jumping out of a moving car, for example). Of course, these thoughts can be a real problem and manifest in harmful ways or be symptomatic of a larger problem.

At times I will imagine this tub of water being filled but never overflowing. The faucet pours a steady stream into the basin but the level of water will not rise. This once occurred in a dream of mine and ever since then, when I happen to consider it, I oftentimes cannot stop. There are so many kinds of repetition in life. Tapping my phone screen until it alights with the time of day or pulling on my earring that is shaped like a lock. Even after the earring broke, I would tug at the flesh for months afterward. When the prophetic words consumed me, they became uncontrollable. I feared them. Felt the need to be in service of them. We create… our own understanding of the world. Golden strands built themselves like houses across the page once I remembered that I could say what I mean. *Lilium columbianum* pooling sweet nectar gelatinous, of the mountainside. Wide-eyed blushing filled under arising brim. A place I imagined but perhaps had never been to. Touch a photo of it. Through my nailbeds amassing green world enveloping the color seen above dimmed thousands of years before time. An eruption and preceding drizzle, pacing, caressing, the song I always thought of the last day of August gold. An impression without dictation.

Language as liberator and liberation; language without the phone screen; language without the bloodlust and void of ethics of the media; language without the United States; language toward a common dream; Zinelli's unceasing language; his language into art; language without a parameter; language as the fabric; language without restriction of meaning or form; sometimes wanting to speak without meaning anything at all; poets thread the needle of the sentence into a weave no one has ever observed before. ✦

✦　✦　✦　✦　✦　✦　✦　✦　✦

I slowly began gaining a sense of other people's religious or spiritual affiliations as I grew older and friendships developed based off things beyond the classroom, in 7-11 parking lots of neighboring towns and on midnight football fields and their forests beyond. I had felt so deeply alienated at that earlier age by being a non-believer. I was looking upon a void. I could not find reasons for human cruelty... how could god will it? I hadn't really read the Bible, the Quran, the Baghavad Gita, the Kojiki...

I yearned for an experience that would coddle me into a collectively architectured philosophy of the world—to be given a perspective by another and know that it was meant to be adapted and adopted into my own DNA. The grace of writers, philosophers, astrophysicists, pianists, composers, artists helped me to build a mind palace. A burgeoning harbor for everything I'd learned. ✦

Robert Rauschenberg. Seven Panel White Painting. 1951. House paint on canvas. 72 x 125 in. (182.9 x 317.5 cm). Robert Rauschenberg Foundation

CHAPTER 17

SOMETIMES I LIKE WRITING ABOUT WORK THAT doesn't feel immediately provocative; even work that annoys me a bit. Here is an artist who has departed the recognizable ground of his artistic practice, searching the shoals and valleys of that which he has not tried and does not know. In the wake of abstract expressionism's emotive intensity came Robert Rauschenberg's reductive White Paintings. So reductive, in fact, that they brought—and still bring—into question how we define art.

My feelings about the artist's work are inextricably tethered to the risks (used lightly!) the artist takes. As I stand before an artwork, as the gentle, initial impressions form a cohesive thought, the first question I ask myself, is *how does it make me feel.*

In August 2017 when the exhibition *Rauschenberg: Among Friends* was on view at the Museum of Modern Art, I finally saw, in person, his famous *White Painting [Seven*

Panel] (1951) in which seven rectangular canvases comprise the larger rectangle of the painting, all rolled with white enamel paint. The demarcations where the canvases are joined are the only obvious inconsistencies on the surface of the monochrome (canvas covered more or less uniformly by the same color). In an absence of color, gesture, representation, I confronted a blank slate. I felt smitten upon first glance, that familiar warm rush to the head. How absorbing to experience an artwork I'd only considered theoretically in reading about abstraction.

A white painting, white light: at the end of the tunnel, or death. White is nothing. It is empty space to be filled. But, emptiness is a vast loneliness, expressing nothing, suggesting everything.

White are our canvases. White are the museum walls of our time; unreflective, unobtrusive, seeming unfeeling, maybe minimizing distractions and reinforce focus. But white can be spilled on, destroyed. White invites shadow, exposing a particle of dust floating around the air in this room, where I become hyperaware of my own spectatorship as my presence, perhaps imperceptibly, changes the light. What would the painting look like if I left?

Much to my chagrin, the two friends I'd giddily brought to the museum that day stood craned over their phones. Their reactions were, however, not unusual, and one should not be bothered by another person's harmless reaction to a work of art. One inevitably hears attempts at humor in front of a piece that any given audience has deemed impenetrable. Perhaps, "I could paint this" or, "a child could do this."

Rauschenberg completed a series of six White Paintings in 1951, comprised of one to seven panels. They've become some of my favorites, but my initial interest in them was piqued by a lack of understanding of what it was that made—and still makes—monochromes such a popular type of painting for artists and spectators alike. Some people dedicate years of study to them; others impulsively reject them. That art can be so polarizing surely makes it worth our curiosity.

There is an urgent need to find the mutual ground within larger disagreements, to transform disconnect into debate. When we poke fun at a painting by questioning its status as a piece of art, we are on the threshold of curiosity. Whatever it is that keeps us from wanting to know more is unnamable. That even the discussion of a particular painting by a particular artist is not considered digestible for a "general audience" gravely underestimates the extent to which that audience can learn from expanded exposure to both old and new work. It is perhaps the case that a general audience is inured by the prevailing media to become content with sound bites and pre-summarized information. This is not meant as an insult and is certainly not revelatory; I am saddened and deeply angered by the idea of a life lived without knowing the emotional and psychological transformations that wonderful works of art provoke.

I recall the times during which a painting transcended my waking hours and drifted into my dreams: I saw a friend who'd died perched aside Louise Bourgeois's *Quarantania* the day I first encountered it at the Whitney, and I gave birth to a girl in my dreams on the humid, heavy summer evening I read of Stella's pregnancy in Tennessee Williams' *A Streetcar Named Desire*. There is an uncanny shiver that courses down the length of my spine when I encounter another person with the same favorite artists. How quickly mind-to-mind vines entangle when people meet each other after independently being moved by the same photograph or story or sculpture. The curvature of my world is bent by art. My experiences of it operate beyond my control.

Some art's worthiness is rarely, if ever, questioned by the public, like Bernini's sculptures or Van Gogh's *Starry Night*. We have absorbed them into our DNA after decades (or hundreds of years) of our consideration have deemed them some of the greatest pieces of art in the Western canon. We find it unhelpful to be contradictory to works with centuries of generally-accepted applause and praise. An aversion to thinking is evident more often during encounters with monochromes, minimalism, and found object. I resist the impulse to say I empathize with this tendency, although I empathize with the frustration of confusion, with sensing, that a painting holds more than it is revealing, or even that something is so visually underwhelming that it bears no need for consideration. I also empathize with the feeling that the path to thinking about art is paved by impenetrable texts and buffered intellectual communities. But, *a refusal to explore on the basis of stubbornness* has led to a large bundle of our contemporary and historical world's brute violence (there is an alleged "loneliness epidemic" among men in America—and not coincidentally the perpetrators of this narrative ignore that we have the highest rate of school shootings in the world, as if men aren't globally lonely—by standards and practices ruled by their own kind). It is too *easy* to look at abstract art and resign oneself to feelings of alienation, stifling the mind's potential for surprise. I think part of this resignation is due to what one expects out of art when she approaches it. Rauschenberg does not turn stone to flesh like Bernini, to be sure. The resemblance of Bernini's works to the three-dimensional human form is immediately recognizable. This ability to sculpt, to master representational detail, is the obvious product of talent and practice and was, for many centuries, the highest achievement of art. Only recently have we reconsidered the application and meaning of representation.

Decontextualized, Rauschenberg's painting would not suggest a particular mastery of form, in the classic sense. Even other monochromes are more sensual. Robert Ryman's *Untitled* (1960) gives us texture, border, a glimpse of the artist's canvas and a gentle suggestion of color some layers within and behind the white paint. Yves Klein's *Blue Monochrome* (1961) is delectable, the blue so blue you can taste it on your tongue, if you stand close enough.

Most people, given a white roller and white paint, could mimic Rauschenberg's painting and no one'd know the difference. The artist, in fact, once gave a curator a paint sample and the work's dimensions in order for him to recreate it for an exhibition overseas. That the White

Paintings have been displayed at the most well-regarded museums and galleries across the world is, to me, a knee-slapper, as I'm always one for harmless antics, particularly when they foster questions about the purpose and role of art.

Rauschenberg's seven-panel *White Painting* is not dazzling (like Klein's blue). A child *could* likely do it, as so many people suggest about monochromes. A child with little art-making experience could likely recreate the painting, certainly if she were given a set of instructions and materials. Roll the paint onto the canvas, make it smooth, cover the surface. The child has the tools to recreate the artwork, but her replica lacks the intent of the original object, just as she, most likely, does not bring the perspective, gleaned from study and practice, that Rauschenberg did to his White Painting series. This comparison is worthy of discussion, but it does not serve to indicate the merits of either work. I am always prepared to accept that enjoying a work for elements beyond the comprehension of a fresh, contextless viewer is kind of ridiculous and pretentious. Alternatively, a White Painting look-alike produced by a child without any prompting would be a different work *entirely* for the simple reason that—contrary to formalist readings, in which the painting is separated from its context—a painting's artist matters to me. The landscape of a life cascades meaning into the work.

When I think about the painting now, I envision its single white color, its even white surface—both serious and a humorous affront, inviting both play and the need for intellectual work. Studying the *White Painting* has made it less important to me whether I like the painting or not, for, I can no longer consider it clearly without the layers of meaning and association that pool in my mind when I see it. The process of discovering is one of creating. The impulse to create—the origin of Rauschenberg's painting—is shared by anyone who has ever hummed a tune to herself while alone in a room, softly breaking silence with a thought which, during its passing through the mind, caught hold and became action.

When Rauschenberg was a young challenger of Modernism, artists decided they were sick of their worth being measured and calculated by the standards set by their dead predecessors. They wanted to banish routine, find a way to communicate how they felt about their contemporary world. They reacted to and expressed human experience. They reshaped and redefined the materials they found around them in daily life. ✦

✦   ✦   ✦   ✦   ✦   ✦   ✦   ✦   ✦

MY PERSONAL SENSE OF TASTE HAS EXPERIENCED THE highs and lows of my contemporary cultures and as I've grown, I see how the things toward which I gravitated as a young(er) person have influenced the ensuing versions of Naomi. I enjoyed finding safety in niche online communities or small fandoms, because those groups felt close and respectful of one another, if not insulated. Today, I find the frenzied consumer culture around commercial books so appalling: it tries to operate in the realm of the tamed. Big Books are only as good as their marketing budget. I think I have finally gained a strong sense of the writing I enjoy. The sentences in those popular books are often ones that have been reformulated over and over again toward recognizability: "It was fun, until it wasn't" or "The main character started walking toward the door, unsure of why she was doing it. And then it struck her..." or "Maybe I'm normal. Maybe I'm insane. Maybe it's both." We all know these formats because they float around like religion, like moons in orbit to be plucked from the author's lexicon at the right moment. They feel comfortable and digestible. Those writers are the popes of publishing. They will get the six-figure advance for these dreary tropes—they can afford to continue on. They will write a narrative that will be the narrative of our time; they will narrativize our time.

In creating, I become a devotee to free-thought. I exceed patterns of dichotomizing and voyeurism. I am saying this mostly to myself like a mantra, and although it is pitiful, perhaps you will agree and that is good. This is not just about loving artwork; it is about adopting patterns of thinking on my own terms, letting the world become a boundless ocean into which I'll plunge. ✦

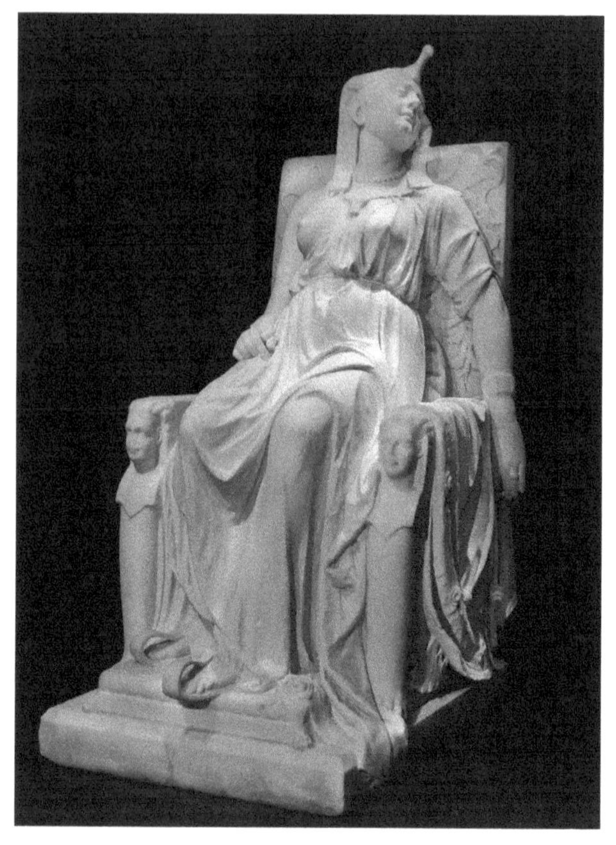

Edmonia Lewis. *The Death of Cleopatra.* Carved 1876. Marble. 63 x 31 1/4 x 46 in. (160.0 x 79.4 x 116.8 cm.) Smithsonian American Art Museum. Gift of the Historical Society of Forest Park, Illinois

CHAPTER 18

AT THE BEGINNING OF WRITING THIS I DID NOT WANT to say that I cannot remember how I first learned of the sculptor named Edmonia Lewis. Hands swoop through meager clouds of haze to grasp my own palm of air. Was I introduced by taking a photo of one of her works? If I was, that photo is lost in the digital graveyard, laid to rest between all the lost iPhone and flip phone libraries all the way back to my first Geocities account. Did I write her name down somewhere in one of my devices, in one of my notebooks? Edmonia Lewis. I want to honor my initial perception of her sculpture by drawing it into a narrative concrete and memorable. Like the account of the first time we met.

And as I've learned more about Lewis, this lack of precision on my end becomes wildly cumbersome. I recently reread Shakespeare's *Antony and Cleopatra*, and I was thinking about Lewis's most famous works depicting *The Death of Cleopatra*. The parameters of ideal sculpture do not usually tend to resonate with me in my limited, contemporary mentality and framework: the idealized body, the technical precision and skill I assume to be afforded a paltry few of the world at the time (and still). I am oftentimes impatient with sculptures that are illegible to me. When I say this, I mean that I cannot read them because they do not strike an emotional chord. As beautiful as they are, I've wandered through the Greek and Roman Art collection at the Met and been blinded by the repetition of political figures I do not recognize (and general heroics). This is undoubtedly my own shortcoming, and it's not to say I don't find them beautiful nonetheless. What I'm writing is all to explain that when I DID see Edmonia Lewis's sculpture at the Smithsonian and stop to investigate it, I knew my interest was exceptional. All the more exceptional because I cannot remember how I recognized her name.

There is not a wide range of published material on Lewis, which was initially a barrier but later became an interesting problem for me as opposed to an obnoxious one. There is a biography by Jeannine Atkins. There is a piece of scholarship by Kirsten Pai Buick: *Child of the Fire: Mary Edmonia Lewis and the Problem of Art History's Black and Indian Subject*. In Buick's work, she beautifully outlines the image of Cleopatra that Lewis would have encountered when she sculpted in the latter half of the nineteenth century. Even by that time, Cleopatra's image had tumbled and twisted through the hands of a vast and global viewership. She was public domain. She'd been championed by so many people eager to identify with her culturally, nationally, ethnically, politically, etc. and otherwise. I do cheer for certain communities to be able to "claim" a representation so potent and so known and so complex. Claiming and re-claiming are so much the fabric of empowerment in this time.

Lewis encountered a Cleopatra in the nineteenth century who, Buick writes, "had been distilled into very specific events in her biography whether true or fabricated... The tale of Cleopatra's suicide defines, if not forecloses her life... Passion was Cleopatra's downfall, and nineteenth-century women scrambled to differentiate themselves from Cleopatra by highlighting her foreignness and her racial heritage as a black African despite her Greek associations as a member of the Ptolemaic dynasty."

I have a hard time trying to understand the facts of the queen when my own impressions of her have been planted by a severe twenty-first century reading—and first meaningful encounter—of her as Shakespeare's purple and hazy queen. My color of feminism is full of mood, power, intellect, radiance, and sometimes debilitating need for self-fulfillment. I want to read that into the play, into every iteration of Cleopatra. I want her to be what I need in a woman; I do this impulsively and not in the interest of truth of scholarship, only in a daydream, this parasocial idolizing in the secret place inside my mind. I envision Cleopatra as nontoxically heroic, lifting her head above the horizon and toward the sky with unrelenting dignity and composure.

The face of Lewis's marble *Cleopatra* appears to me more multifaceted than tragic. The weaponed and fabled (and debated) asp does not clamp upon her breast or settle around her bicep. Her Antony is not draped across her lap. There is no agony contorting or skewing the features of her face, which has fallen back with chin lifted above the left shoulder. There is no climax to be found here. Cleopatra plants herself atop the throne to signal the beginning of her departure from the fleshly world; the object itself also signifying a moment of change in political history. I wonder if she has a sense of what lay beyond, if anything. She does not stoop or tilt, but rather, sits back into death in preparation for the single largest transition of her years: from here to wherever *that* is.

A sliver part in her lips and slackening and unfurling of her finger joints: the arrival of death is barely announced. Feet firmly planted on the ground of this leafy earth. But ones reading all depends on how one sees death. Only the living are allowed to debate how the dead appear, even if the discussion of it hurts us. In Lewis's sculpture, it is calm like a garden of light; the pure unknown; seeing into the secret blissful dimensions at the end of the road that were previously ungraspable.

Lewis's sculpture was met with excitement upon its reveal in 1876 at the Philadelphia Centennial Exposition. It was a work she'd spent time saving funds for in order to create. There are layers to writing about any work of art if you're a writer who also wants to discuss the artist behind it. Buick describes the tautological treatment of an artist's work as one that—in few words—takes the artist to *be* the artwork. It takes the artwork as being a way to read the artist: it is an act of repetition. I want to take this point into consideration when moving so fluidly between a person and her work.

I do not attempt to draw a parallel between Lewis and Cleopatra by saying their identities have been imprecisely handled. I could tie a stronger parallel between the legacies of Cleopatra and Mary Magdelene in how the West has, for centuries, worked hard to identify them as feminine enemies of the patriarchy.

When I say that Lewis's image is also enigmatic to me, it is because I was curious about her upon first investigating her and because reading about her has only deepened my curiosity about her. The first time I googled Lewis, the location of her gravesite was still unknown. It was really odd to me that this was the case; I held onto that factoid. So, it was an incredible moment of self-doubt when I began researching her years later and found her burial site listed as the very first search result and clearly as being in London. The Internet is always changing. I always forget. The location had been brought into public consciousness because her biographer Marilyn Richardson had shed light on it! Scholarship keeps us blazing across centuries. As I get older, I increasingly feel myself a part of history, as opposed to a quiet witnesser of it. Peering through the years. This was a moment that underscored the sentiment.

Buick presents a number of complicated reasons for the falsities that riddle many attempts to document Edmonia Lewis, including Lewis's own "gloss[ing] over unpleasantness in order to recast her biography."

So, there is a certain command of narrative you assume when you represent an existing someone in your artwork or writing: meaning, I'd really like to avoid being Naomi portraying Edmonia Lewis portraying Cleopatra. But, I do think about any artist's motivations, and for someone who seemed so deliberate in the information she let fly into the public sphere (you can see this outlined in other materials; it is fascinating to see which details of her personal life she planted and which she did not... it reads as powerful), I am particularly curious about what she'd have said about Cleopatra. What would she have said to a friend and what would she have said to a reporter? I can't help my curiosity. As I child I loved to imagine certain historical or celebrity figures in their day-to-day operations.

How much can I understand how others see me? I think we can agree that we hope others get us right, that they do not misunderstand our intentions. I imagine watching myself from some godly position, perhaps equipped with a vision that extends beyond "seeing" and into unknown ways of perceiving. One thing my life has proved is that every expression I release into the world is still my secret to keep. No one can read us. The stories others tell of us can never exist in place of us and what we leave behind is really... all there is. ✦

✦ ✦ ✦ ✦ ✦ ✦ ✦ ✦ ✦

It can be sophomoric to rage against the indus-try without an antidote. Deep in the catacombs of my mind I store the language of Nathaniel Dorsky in his speech-turned-essay entitled "Devotional Cinema," which came to me unexpectedly as I skimmed through a publication about film and faith at the request of an-other institution who wanted to republish part of it in their own book. Dorsky defines devotional cinema as a work that "subverts our absorption in the temporal and reveals the depths of our own reality, it opens us to a fuller sense of ourselves and our world. It is alive as a devotional form." Devotional work makes us cry, aspire, dream, dance, rage. His philosophy is transferrable to any medium. In devotional writing, perhaps the author aims to make use of language's materiality (the things we learn in high school—subtext, poetic devices, experimenta-tion). It is what distinguishes, for example, the writing of Chika Sagawa from the banality of a narrative Jonathan Franzen-like writer. There many like the latter but none especially akin the former. I mean to make a distinction between a writer making an experiment and a writer writ-ing a story. It's not that I assume bestselling fiction guilty before innocent—just yearning for something different, always, something where the writer can be sensed in every detail of the words and how they were alchemized onto the page. If you hate that statement just remind yourself it's my opinion (so is this whole book). I love to debate. But plenty of storywriters can do both: they write an experiment told through a story. Some write a story told through an experiment. Both their voices are plunged deeply into the structure and vocabulary of my own writing. I adore them so.

I do not know how a sensibility for language or art comes to be. I enjoy imagining each person's design; all the components that come together to form the human before me. ✦

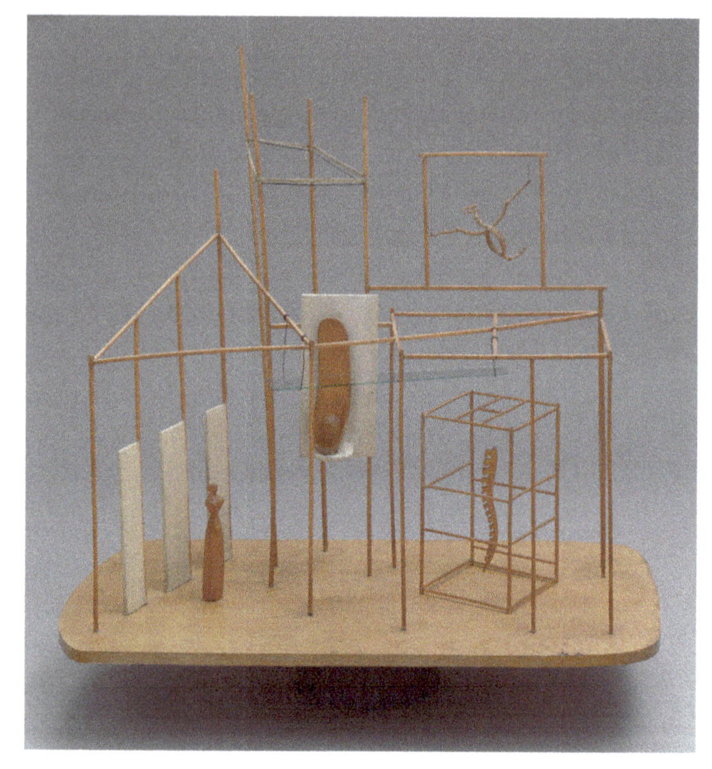

Alberto Giacometti (Swiss, 1901–1966). *The Palace at 4 AM*. 1932. Wood, glass, wire, and string. 25 x 28 ¼ x 15 ¾ in. (63.5 x 71.8 x 40 cm). The Museum of Modern Art, New York. Purchase

CHAPTER 19

I came to revisit Giacometti's modernist house on a difficult day and left enlightened; emboldened to write the book that you are reading at this moment in time. It has been one of my favorite works of art for as long as I can remember; since I was a girl far away from New York City with books of art on my shelves.

I was feeling a significant pain from a broken relationship. A portal had closed without warning, and it was only the beginning of the cold months in New York. Like so many Americans who have had a lifetime of depending on the late-capitalistic structure of my life to dull out the sharpness of feelings from "personal" dramas, I've a tendency to disregard a chasm forming in my interiority by hurling myself into emails and meetings, finding solace in busywork and general meaninglessness in the face of larger life changes. It's okay to take your mind off things, sometimes, I guess. Woke up to remember I was sad. Got my usual coffee at the bodega and I almost shed tears when I spilled some on the counter. Rode the J over the bridge, transferred to the M, listened to some Ravel. Sometimes it helps, other times it's too familiar to jolt me out of it. Got my second coffee in the staff cafeteria, slumped at my desk. Stared at my phone for a little bit and clicked around my apps.

I was impossibly restless, so before the museum opened, I walked down to the galleries. We'd just had our big re-opening in autumn 2019, and I was still unfamiliar with the expansion and all that the rooms offered. The gallery painted dark purple with all the Surrealist works never failed me. There I found my favorite strange little building, a bonelike midcentury charm: Alberto Giacometti's *The Palace at 4 A.M.* Although the Museum's mission was to reconfigure its stance toward the canon it created in the twentieth century, certain beloved works remained on display and were possibly even more prominent than before. I was used to seeing this Giacometti near Meret Oppenheim's furry *Object*, but it was nice to see, for example, a recently-acquired Remedios Varo painting join the company. *The Palace*'s changing environment was testament to how many times I'd been to the Museum, even before being employed by it.

The Palace at 4 A.M. is a wood sculpture with glass, wire, and string details. Its architecture is sparse, thin, upright, and geometric, but not tough. At any moment it would be crushed under the weight of a devastating story or the gust of a summer afternoon's humid wind. It has a gentle lack of continuousness, like a duet of fingerpicked guitars playing different songs in the same chord. You can point out the rooms. I always smile to see how a few small sculptures occupy the house. They're vaguely similar to—though seemingly emotionally lighter than—the artist's standalone ones and are either hung on the wood scaffolding or suspended between it. Giacometti does have a few toylike, gamelike sculptures, but most of his work tends toward the macabre. This work eludes Post-War devastation; it is an exception. It is so autonomous, but so important to me how it rounds out his work, that any retrospective of his that lacks it feels starkly incomplete although I know most art critics would probably argue with me on that (I don't care). The outliers of an artist's body of work are always provoking us to investigate, to wonder why someone strayed from their routine. I sense others are drawn to *The Palace* for reasons similar to mine: it really does remind of a dollhouse! One might pause upon finding a recognizable-ish object in a roomful of surrealism, of objects not meant to be seen together.

I was full of tears that morning in November and was glad no one was around to see it. I go through periods of being easily moved by art, whether or not I'm particularly blue. I ruminated for a few minutes in the gallery before returning to my desk through the inconspicuous staff entrance to the elevator, whereupon I had a quick conversation with my colleague Sophie and returned to my desk. My colleague also happened to be one of my closest friends, and a few minutes later she sent me a brief bit of scholarship about *The Palace* that we'd published on our website. It quotes Giacometti's own thoughts on the sculpture, which resulted from a half-year love affair:

"We constructed a fantastical palace in the night," he wrote, "… a very fragile palace of matches; at the least false movement a whole section of the diminutive construction would collapse; we would always begin it all over again."

The idea that matchsticks serve one purpose but were used for another is already charming and impulsive and playful, especially for an artist who did not work with found object. The work is a bit craftlike. Even more sweet is how closely this romance was replicated into his work, how seriously it was handled. The story deviates from the godlike severity usually reserved to characterize the -ism celebrities of the 20th century. To say something is all of these things (sweet, charming, domestic) is not to suggest that they're without depth. I like to use these words in power to readdress their historical meanings and shed light on their avenues for expression.

The Palace's rooms are merely suggestions of separated space. I find their meaning elusive. As an architectural model can only ever suggest the experience of traveling the interior of a built structure, the sculpture is a sketch of a place. It actually does look like a drawing if you view it at eye-level, from afar, flattened by its angularity. I think that its contents are reserved for the lovers; the rooms are the domain of those under the influence of co-dependency. Like a palace, a love cannot be known from the outside looking in.

I think of the failure of a joint effort such as the matchstick palace built by Giacometti and Denise (full name unfortunately unknown), and of how it can be met with the opportunity to rebuild, and of how the writer Mina Hamedi once wrote that things must fall apart to come back together again in a operatic and tempestuous cycle of life. I wonder what variations might have been implemented in each version of the sculpture's prototype.

I suppose the best parts were crystallized in the artist's final work, to be seen forever. A palace holds the promise of grandiosity, a place that we can visit but never have for ourselves. There are dark places within, like a cistern, where a mystery lives, though from the outside you'd never know. And I'd never want something so lavish; I'd get lost. You want to know where someone is when you shout for them at home. But Giacometti's palace—it is simply the residence of someone important without the ruckus. It is given meaning by those it symbolizes.

194After I left work, I went to get Japanese curry for dinner with the artist Dylan Reitz in Greenpoint. I remember how cold it was that evening. We had some catching up to do, and I explained to him how odd my day had been, and we talked about how days of emotional unrest are oftentimes revealing. The stark contrast between a personal sadness and the identification you might feel with someone else's work of art is such a chance encounter, so dependent on so many circumstances, like love. The ensuing discussions about art—and how our relationships are deepened through them—are perhaps more important than the ones we have with ourselves. You see, I felt an invisible string of knowledge form between myself and my dear friends I'd seen that day. It was a delicious dinner, and by the time I got home I felt like the past fourteen hours had been a pilgrimage. I began to watch a sweet autumnal spooky Americana animated show Dylan had recommended and it further emboldened how important the characters of our lives are in shaping the course of our days. ✦

$\ast$ $\ast$ $\ast$ $\ast$ $\ast$ $\ast$ $\ast$ $\ast$ $\ast$

THE WORDS IN MY HEAD GREW QUIET FOR A MOMENT; twenty-six characters funneling toward oblivion, back to whence they came. Peace seeking; internal light finding. The end-of-story calm of a bronzed fall evening. If I could write a letter to you, I'd tell you that you'll be in my flower garden of perennials forever. ✦

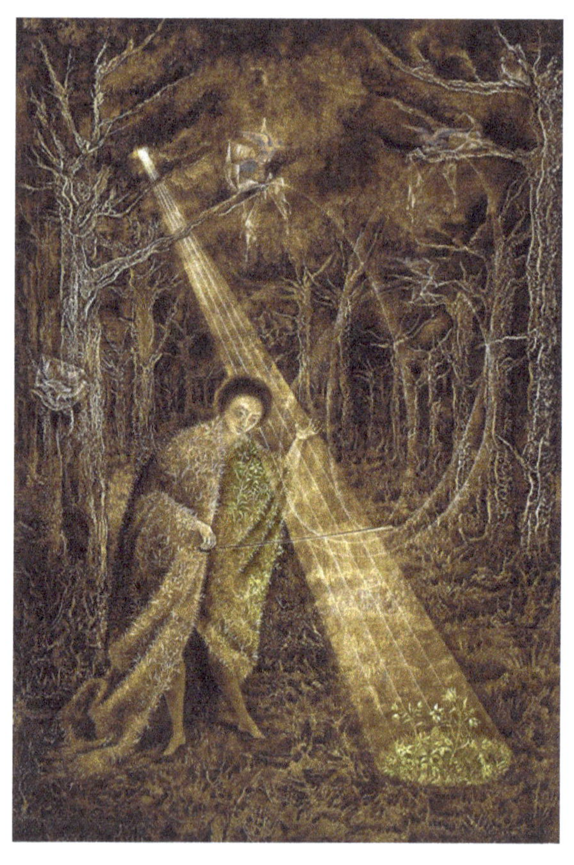

REMEDIOS VARO (SPANISH, 1908–1963). *Música solar (Solar Music)*. 1955. OIL ON HARDBOARD. 5 13/16 x 24 IN. (91 x 61 CM). PRIVATE COLLECTION

CHAPTER 20

REMEDIOS THE ALCHEMIST, REMEDIOS THE BEWITCH-
ing. Her own practice was one that shot across horizons,
mixing media and systems, applying wondrous and varying schools of thought.

She's been having a small heyday for the past several years,
along with her best friend Leonora Carrington who is another artist I adore (since I began writing this, they've just
had a gorgeous show of her work at Art Institute of Chicago in 2023). They've both had volumes published of letters and stories and tarot decks. Carrington has not found
her way into this book, but her work sticks with you, and
for anyone reading this I would suggest her slim volume
entitled *Down Below* to which my own work is indebted.

Born in Madrid, Varo spent time in Paris as a young
adult, but ultimately fled Spain to return to France when
the Spanish Civil War broke out, before eventually ar-
riving in Casablanca and waiting to relocate to Mexico,

where she experienced a prolific period of work and remained until her death. She passed away at just fifty-four
from a heart attack. And after having staged only two solo
exhibitions, I sense the work that has been done to continue her legacy is due to so many women who are curators and writers and thinkers in the world who want to
make sure the books get things right—to make sure that
she is fleshed out in her narrative, that she is expressed
expansively, that works about tether her wide range of artistic and personal pursuits and intellectual circles. I am
grateful for them. How else would I have stumbled upon
this work without the elegant scholarship that opens the
floodgates to reception?

The palette of Varo's dusty magnificence is robed in
earthen shades of pumpkin, slate, evergreen, sapphire, and
all of it slightly kissed by grey. Her scenes depict an hour-
less realm where moon and sun do not disperse light in
an intuitive sense. Something between Earth and beyond.
Recognizable only in dreams, accessible via transcendence
or possibly not at all to anyone except the artist herself.
An atmospheric gloom hindering the blazing torch of
high noon, much like the hazy fantasy worlds of the '90s
and '00s (see films like *Mirrormask* [2005] or games such
as the singular work of art that is *American McGee's Alice*

[2000]). The composition of some of her work is akin to the symphonic bizarre of Hieronymus Bosch (I see many other people make this comparison on the web) or near-contemporary Pieter Bruegel the Elder; with scenes sometimes drawn back into a very slightly tilted omniscience, either from above or below but never declaratively.

Música solar depicts a grassy-robed person peering upon a patch of blooming flowers in the woods, illuminated by a singular, alien ray of light which extends from a place beyond the cloud cover darkening the wanderer's world. The ray is sectioned by stringlike threads, which the wanderer plays using a bow. The Art Institute of Chicago published *Remedios Varo: Science Fictions* in 2023, a catalogue with attentive production (including a gate fold of Varo's triptych) and excellent close readings of works in the show. Art historian and curator Claire Howard discusses the blending of science and music at play between "the Pythagorean theory of the music of the sphere's and [George] Gurdjieff's musical metaphor for creation," the latter in which the Ray of Creation includes varying rates of vibration attributed to different spheres which produce unique sounds (this is a bit of an oversimplification). What we have at play is Varo's investigation and manifestation of forces unseen, perhaps often unsensed.

There is a search for interconnectedness and cosmic order.

(I have to note here that I have never seen this painting in real life, and I am actually not sure where it lives; the former is a cardinal sin of writing about art and I do not care. There are shortcomings to writing about art at this kind of distance, and every writer who has attempted it would likely lament these if you asked. The experience of art IRL is a luxury; it demands our time, access, physical ability, knowledge, and is gatekept by so many monolithic industries, that witnessing it usually comes with a price tag. Works in private collections (where this painting resides), are only viewable if the collector has loaned it to an exhibition, donated it to a museum, auctioned it, or otherwise made their collection open to our curious eyes. Such is the nature of a work that is a one of one... books are objects printed and sometimes reprinted, consumed en masse and collectively living across the spaces and centuries of our Earth. New editions arise, fresh translations are rendered, language might morph and change truer to the author's intent or at times away from it. We bring books back into print if they lose their way and aim to shape, correct, brighten history by the course of our work as book publishers.)

Lines, threads, and other mysterious connective and transitional tissues appear all over her paintings and certainly in *Música solar.* In a note written about her 1956 painting *Armonía (Harmony)*, she wrote "the character is trying to find the invisible thread that unites all things" regarding her subject who constructs a line of music in the air. The thread and the wanderer's string seem compatible. You'll find countless examples of these transformative lines in this period of her work. She wrote down delightful recipes for dreams and formulas that explained the world.

The wanderer's world is a place whose everlasting brownness is elemental and therefore a life source. In fact, nothing verifiably green in sight as even the blooming flower is starched in musical alchemy. And the forest behind is like the reflection one sees of oneself while standing between an infinity mirror. It is unclear whether or not it leads anywhere at all or is contained within some strange bend of space. Endlessness can only ever be suggested and never witnessed.

Sometimes I have this dream, in which a slight incline below my feet brings me to a cliff over the sea. Its surface is whitecapped and I see rain approach from offshore, and with it, a door. The door washes toward me on the surface of the ocean, unjolted by what appears to me a rough tide.

It's otherworldly, as am I. I raise my left wrist away from my hip and half-circle it toward the sky, because I want the door to come closer. It rises, continuing to lay flat. Once it reaches the edge of the cliff, it swings open, and I am left with a decision to either escape limbo or not… I thought this place would be a void, not a *who* with purpose and feeling. The sensation of lucidity, agency, or awareness within a dream is nearly indescribable. It reminds me of Surrealism because when it happens, the dreamscape becomes a playground, an experiment. A place where you can approach Death not in the sense of Death as finality, but perhaps in a sense of Death as an entrypoint. I believe that Remedios Varo knew this.

I took a course on memorials once a week when I was in college, and I attended dutifully, motivated to impress the young philosophy professor. His constant exasperation intrigued me, and I'd made myself happy by imagining his devotion to serious philosophical thought. I wanted to be that smart or care that much about anything.

I'd always worked hard for teachers who devastated me in one way or another, opening portals of depth and emotional complexity and introducing me to feelings beyond the ones I'd encountered in most of daily life. One time, during a blue period, a professor called me into his office to tell me I looked wan, and wrote down the addresses of several of the closest and freshest produce purveyors. One teacher closed her eyes with arms outstretched for just a moment too long when embodying Ophelia's river suicide in front of the class. Another cried in remembering her dead sister while reading aloud from *Pedro Paramo*. Another, perhaps the most influential of all, gave me a copy of Sontag's *Regrading the Pain of Others*. I wanted to be sure that human life was as tempestuous or arbitrary as it seemed. Anything that underscored my suspicion was comforting. I needed space to observe my feelings with care.

Anyway, that November morning in the classroom in upstate New York, my five-o'clock-shadowed professor told us we'd need to write him a paper describing our own hypothetical memorials. We'd spent the time in class that semester discussing public memory, so this final direction to point the eye inward was a proper way to wrap it up. At that age, I'd expressed several times that I felt our postcolonial American collective memory oftentimes stifled, circled, and entrapped the dead, but I didn't know much beyond a feeling of revulsion (now, of course, turn to chapter 9/11 to understand why Americans my age might struggle with this). He had a friend whose wife had passed away several years ago. Professor's recounting of this narrative was lean; it spared many details in lieu of getting to the point. This person added his deceased's ashes to his breakfast in the morning. A warm tide rose behind my eyes. I didn't want to show emotion, self-conscious about public displays of empathy. How infrequently were such intimacies disclosed in a room full of strangers? All I could manage was to ask him how he found out, but he only raised his palm. I thought about this for days, it stuck with me for years. The story begs consideration, but my professor's choosing to share it—and without explanation—felt like he'd given a clue.

206   Perhaps he was showing the limitless nature of memorialization, that it could be constructed down multitudinous avenues. I think I associate with his general life position now more closely than before, and I read his anecdote as a shriek into the pillow. When one becomes encapsulated in the narrative of his life, what might otherwise seem bizarre becomes quotidian. Like all the behaviors we turn to when livelihood is compromised. I can too easily imagine (as I'm sure you can, too).

We are always only one thread away from recalibration, surreality is written into art to capture the things we cannot do or say in response to what we know or see. What

I am saying is that I understand. The memory of this peculiarity is just one door of endless memory doors I walk by when I sit down to write. Pull the handle; slouch and stumble through. I did it so often without thinking about the possibilities or limitations of the space I entered.

In Varo's work, memory is somewhat undefined. Perhaps any painting can be a memorial. Her work is objectively less concerned with death and more with explanation, the bringing of the unseen into visual representation in which the sonic and microcosmic realities of human fabric play a slow and long sound. A sound like a river of words unceasing.

207

The spheres of death, memorialization, dreamspace, and interpretations. Together they pose the only question that gets to the essence of being human: do I choose to continue life? Death and dreaming aren't so different to me. The decision gapes before me as if eager to swallow me. There's the ocean, its waves so seductively and I wouldn't mind staying in limbo forever if it meant I could bob upon a surface I gazed at with longing so often in my life. But why choose to continue falling when I've been presented with an option. I'd try something new if it meant I could influence the outcome. I'm not sure what nothingness holds, surely no story no matter how fantastical could have prepared me to confront this. ✦

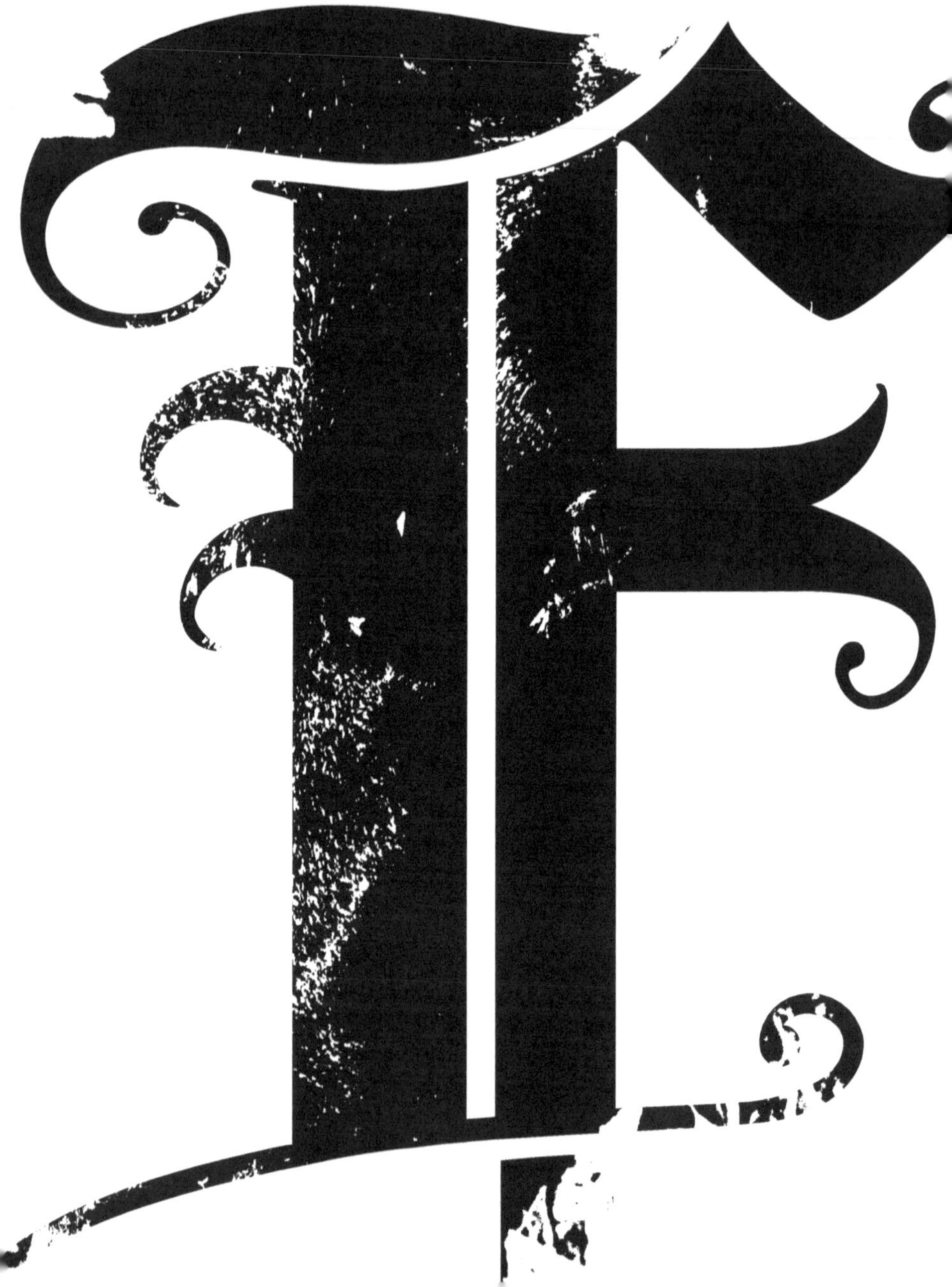

F I N

A few days' visit to the morgue didn't give me the answers but I got them from the memories of the things I had seen. People say they die and come back to life; I cannot know. The limbo I travelled was only in dreams: through the forests and oceans of my subconscious. We experience such a range of little, non-literal deaths. A fiery blaze of ash and isolation. Fading of spirit and reignition of pain, identity loss and the moment you fail to recognize yourself in the mirror. When did twenty years go by? And how came the purpose to create?

When big Death comes it is profound and it is the end. It is what is guaranteed and sacred because it is the only experience we will not collect in our memories to pile on with other memories. The thing I cannot write about. The fact of its occurrence is transferred to those who—if we are privileged enough to have them—know that we lived. I used to be crushed by the hypothesis that I had some grand idea to make the world "better" but that I would leave behind only a long pattern of different lonelinesses and alienations and embarrassments—having grown up widely perceived on the web, for example, broadcasting my feelings and doubts too much. As I write this now, I am unconvinced that there is a direct purpose to my writing practice. It is a series of question that are addressed each day anew, sometimes affirmed and sometimes denied but mostly ignored. It feels like I face a huge and demanding audience of one million Naomi's who do not wave back, who do not laugh with me but observe.

Writing as witness... Then I think of all the senseless, unthinkable Death we inflict on each other, with our machinations of war and destruction and our minds sickened by capitalism and corruption. Larger and larger problems outside the insignificant things I've got to say. My small life—how paltry. These words—so general. I feel as if I must apologize for them and therefore for existing, for having the audacity to use language as a tool of expression. I arrive at the platform from which I'd left, so devastated by the predictable circle of my life.

And here I am now, still, knowing nothing. But now, in some arbitrary break from the cycle, bliss arrives where the assignation of meaning ends, when the art can mean everything rather than anything. Where I can say what I feel. Sometimes now I sing until I cry and sometimes I want to be alone. And mostly I yearn to be alone. I only write sometimes. I rub the dirt of sadness into my hair and cast atheistic spells on people I love. Going deeper into the heart of a feeling instead of letting it simmer. Take everything to be art until proven innocent. I'm screaming into the bathtub because it brings me clarity. I look outside. Sometimes you have to run away. Things become warmer. Somewhere there's a light.

The appendages of memory untangle and separate upon my confrontation of them, until they hover about me like stillborn snakes. Past them is nothing but space, field of unvaried carnelian. Chaos settles and leaves a psychological framework for understanding feelings instead of observing them as they fly overhead. When my blood was spilled by the words it replaced the air around me and began to expand unflinchingly. The body rebuilt itself anew.

Reborn perhaps for the first time or maybe I'm only noticing it this time around. The condition of our planet and its inhabitants had seemed brimming with fact and my place within the system was like a path up the mountainside. Trudging along, mistaking time for opportunity and filling it with notions of productivity and definition. It is the case that we can stab at a description of what we see, but that even if you and I agree on the general point it's more likely than not that we will fail to produce an identical portrait. Art told me that. And it helped me begin to understand how to read language and faces, gestures and caresses.

My interpretation of art is certainly contingent on my systems of nonbelief, but I have always been enraptured by the other people's ideas about spirituality, in their conviction that an outside or higher power configures into the chaos and order of their lives. On how the religious perceive death as some kind of bridge or passage. So much of my life has been spent wondering what it would be like to have this dependency, this certainty in being held accountable for your actions and knowing the price you must pay for them via the outlining of a religious text.

And even without God, I am still full of devotion.

A final memory: I am fidgeting in the pew on Sunday morning, looking through the pages of the bible, and I always loved how fragile they were. Almost translucent. I behold the language on the pages with joy; I dip in and out of understanding the contents. Such musicality and tonality. That year, my fourth-grade teacher had asked me why I wanted to do a book report on Charles Dickens, and I told her it reminded me of the King James bible.

The pastor has finally arrived at the end of the sermon. I hadn't been listening, having always found him and his unadorned Lutheran pulpit underwhelming and disturbing. A simulation of sorts, like the flattened renderings of an N64. Behind him, a huge window exposes the field behind the church, so that is another thing I do as I wait for this to be over. I look out. Nothing of particular excitement occurring beyond the field and the street and the gate to the suburban neighborhood and its multi-car garages. The trees don't rustle. Nothing is agitated out there today. Strange. My city in the sea, on some days. The delivery of the sermon was without fire and consequence. Language without direction is how I see it now. Who knows what I thought then, but I'm still the same girl. I dreamt of the meadow in the woods behind my house and how I'd like to read a book there and have a picnic with my best friend because it would be sunnier and green outside soon…

After filing out of the pews, grandmothers stand in rows on either side of the double-doors, handing us palm fronds. I am small and the palms arch over me, and I am in the passageway of the trees, mighty corridor for just a moment. I carry my frond toward the red exit sign, surprised at the slightness of its stem, tender like a mouse's ribcage. I want to protect it. When I emerge from the tunnel, the lobby is filled with noon light, and the room, which is usually flat and sallow, is luminescent—as if reflecting moving water—against people dressed so finely. What troubles me about this memory is that I know it is inaccurate. When I drive by that church now, when I recall the lobby of it on any other day, it is ungraced by holy visions or even the possibility for magnificent thought. It was a small room with fold-out tables and Ficus trees and yellowing tiles. The ceiling was paneled and the walls were sallow and bare. It could not have been so bright and so big. Everyone was scandalized when they found out the pastor used the community offerings to pay a mortgage on his house. During Sunday School we watched Veggie Tales. I only ever remember being bored.

But the vision comes to me in ethereal swatches and explosive tones like a reckoning. My mother hands me her palm frond, and now I have two. I fan them above my head, squinting to see the way they move like feathers in the water. They are unbelievably green. That I'd been neither baptized nor crowned by any religion crossed my mind; it often did when I was here. Once I'd come close to letting it happen. I remember sitting in the pastor's office asking about the part with the pool. His room was too narrow and rectangular—like a coffin—and I felt uncomfortable. But, today seemed like it would have been the right day for it, a baptism—in this golden light, dipped back into unstirring water, in this golden light, a birth in the afternoon. The gleam from the buckle on an old man's shoe caught my eye. The room was enrobed in the brightest glow I'd ever seen. I took my mother's hand. I had to close my eyes and reopen them over and over again until they adjusted. Golden incandescence dipped in violet of the divine. A fissure in the very crust of the earth, enveloping me into the Kingdom. Let your eyes toward the sky and be told answers. They are promised and will come to you and enchant you. The later hours will pass and eventually be shut off. Everything around your body dilates under your time and direct interaction. Close your eyes and imagine the bowing curvature of the planet Earth. A sphere of damp clay being shaped by two hands tells you about time and memory. The clay is like prose; the prose you write will step through the doors of the palace and into the sun rising with you, and you will throw your hands toward it. This is symphonic creation; everything galloping together at once. Toward some undocumented plain. There are times when I've seen it. It comes to me more and more as I do this; using the words as a net to gather the meaning of my life; I say violet but see lavender and thistle; how to express it. Perhaps it sounds sad. Irredeemable. Though the inability to retrieve something is sweet, too. Strange currents of life rushing between your fingers; writing attempting to capture it but never quite getting it right.

The most beautiful images of childhood are fraught with longing, because you know that earlier versions of yourself, more ignorant versions, were unburdened by the years to come. ✦

ACKNOWLEDGMENTS

To Mina Hamedi, the fabric of my world, who believed in this book without question, who took a risk on representing my project and without whom it wouldn't have been written.

To John Trefry, for seeing what I see and championing this book. Inside the Castle is a singular project and I am humbled by my inclusion in its incomparable list. To Mike Corrao for his beautiful typesetting.

To Leyla Hamedi for her exquisite eye.

To Chris Molnar for everything. To Nicodemus Nicoludis for his unshakeable strength and poems. To the both of them, who have embarked on the mission of publishing books with me, which been one of the most transformative experiences of my life. Archway Editions published a very early version of this book's introduction.

To Ki Smith for his years of mentorship, for allowing me to journey with him through the glories and perils of running a gallery.

To Ryan Bock, my coconspirator in a shadowy world.

To Sophie Golub for being my early and devoted reader.

To Dylan Reitz for having ramen with me on the night which inspired the final form of this project.

To Chukwuma Ndulue whose limitless poetry provoked the final pages of my book.

To all the artists in this book who have opened their studios and minds to me.

To Jessi Lembo, my moon.

To Mia Risher for lovingly spreading the propaganda of this book.

To my creative collaborators and writers and friends who were present during the formation of this work: Forrest Xavier Lockhart, Ivana Djiya, José Carpio, Sergio

Romanello, Annina Roescheisen, Sabrina Otness, Katrina Passarella, Richie Quake, Nifath Chowdhury, Anya Lewis-Meeks, Sima Safavi-Bayat, Ryan Meehan, Mark Meneses, Etan Nechtin, Lexi French, Matt Varner, Sarah-Jane Collins, Nicholas Goodly, Mathews Huey, Caroline McManus, Allegra Pagano, Chris Blackman, Tyler Green, Jean Frazier, Hans Koennecke, Zeynep Özakat, Jakob Guanzon, Mina Seçkin, Will Meyer, Colin Denlinger, Jared Daniel Fagan, Claire Donato, Nik Slackman, charles theonia, Ereka Imani Duncan, Hank Jost, Tony Cousins, Lindsey Webb, Amy Griffis, Terry Nguyen, Alex Garner, Nick Greer, Ava María, Anton Bitter, Kelsey Niziolek, Artem Velycko, Mitchell Hendricks, Vlad Mamai, Justine Pierre, Yarik Svyrdenko, Ketterick Waddell, Liz Janoff, Kazi, Corey Allen, Josh Allen, Nas Leber, Al Porto, Brandon Blue, Charlie Hudson, Mike McKeever, Britne Oldford, Justin Orvis Steimer, Ninette Golub, Leslie Finnie, Iris O'Flaherty, Andy Zalkin, Sirena He, Hunter Hodkinson. To Sydnie Hyams and Nica Mayer, my new comrades in publishing. To all the people of nightlife and literature. For anyone I've missed here I'm sorry.

To Alan Gilbert for teaching me about poetry and publishing my work on art for many years.

To past and present MoMA Publications folks who were around for the significant moments of this books creation: Hannah Kim, Marc Sapir, Emily Hall, Amanda Washburn, Jackie Neudorf, Rebecca Roberts, Bryan Stauss, Matthew Pimm, and Don McMahon.

To Daniel Power for his trust in my collaborative visions for our beautiful books and for expanding my understanding of photography.

To Michael Greenberg, who has shaped my work as a writer of nonfiction.

To my extraordinary high school English and history teachers: Mr. Costello, Ms. Oglesby, Mrs. Bowker, Mrs. Russell. To my world-shaping professors: Silvio Torres-Saillant, Eileen Schell, Phillip Lopate, Leslie Jamison, Wayne Koestenbaum. To Richard Locke, rest in peace.

To Mike and Aillene Paull, for their support and love.

To Ivan Tsukanov, the dark lord of music and sound.

To Beverly Terry, I dedicate this book to you.

To Matthew Falk, my brother and protector and voice of light in a difficult world. To Lisa Dimak, the sister of my dreams.

And to Anne and Philip Falk, the guiding night sky of my essence and creation.

ART CREDITS

Epidemie by Alfred Kubin: © Eberhard Spangenberg, München / Artists Rights Society (ARS), New York, 2025

Untitled by Louise Bourgeois: © 2025 The Easton Foundation / Licensed by VAGA at Artists Rights Society (ARS), NY. Courtesy MoMA, NY, Imaging and Visual Resources, Denis Doorly.

Going Around the Corner Piece by Bruce Nauman: © 2025 Bruce Nauman / Artists Rights Society (ARS), New York

Trojan Gates by Helen Frankenthaler: © 2025 Helen Frankenthaler Foundation, Inc. / Artists Rights Society (ARS), New York . Photo courtesy MoMA, NY, Imaging and Visual Resources, John Wronn.

The Four Seasons (Spring) by Wendy Red Star: Wendy Red Star. Spring, 2006. Archival pigment print on Sunset Fiber rag. 21 x 24 in. (53.3 x 70 cm). Courtesy of the artist. © Wendy Red Star

Reclining Woman on Sofa by Gregory Crewdson: © Gregory Crewdson

Canyons of Streets by Yukio Morinaga: Yukio Morinaga (1888–1968). Canyon of Streets. C. 1925. Gelatin silver print. 13 3/8 x 10 1/8 in. (34 x 25.7 cm). Private Collection, Courtesy of Cascadia Art Museum, Edmonds, WA.

Untitled by Carlo Zinelli: © photo credit Collection de l'Art Brut, Lausanne, Morgane Détraz, Atelier de numérisation

Seven Panel White by Robert Rauschenberg: © 2025 Robert Rauschenberg Foundation / Licensed by VAGA at Artists Rights Society (ARS), NY

The Palace at 4 by Alberto Giacometti: © Succession Alberto Giacometti / Artists Rights Society (ARS), NY, 2025. Courtesy MoMA, NY, Imaging and Visual Resources, Thomas Griesel.

Solar Music by Remedios Varo: © 2025 Remedios Varo, Artists Rights Society (ARS), New York / VEGAP, Madrid